PAPERCRAFTING
with Donna Dewberry

PAPERCRAFTING
with Donna Dewberry

NORTH LIGHT BOOKS

North Light Books
Cincinnati, Ohio
www.artistsnetwork.com

ABOUT THE artist

For years, Donna Dewberry has been respected in the decorative painting world, and now she has become a popular household name as well. Donna is devoted to creating art by developing new techniques that make painting and decorating accessible to everyone. She has successfully shared her love of creating with painters and crafters everywhere through her One-Stroke painting method and her continually new ideas.

Creating books of "scraps" and memories is a favorite hobby of Donna's. She has a large family of her own, and it is a way for her to share her family stories and memories with others. Donna lives with her wonderful family in Florida, where she paints and spends as much time as possible with her husband, seven children and seven grandchildren.

09 08 07 06 05   5 4 3 2 1

Library of Congress Cataloging-in-Publication Data
Dewberry, Donna S.
   Papercrafting with Donna Dewberry / by Donna Dewberry.-- 1st ed.
       p. cm.
   Includes index.
   ISBN 1-58180-673-6 (pbk.)
   1. Greeting cards. 2. Scrapbooks. 3. Painting--Technique. 4.
Decoration and ornament. I. Title.
   TT872.D48 2005
   745.7'23--dc22

Editors: Jessica Gordon, Christine Doyle
Designer: Karla Baker
Layout Artist: Kathy Gardner
Production Coordinator: Robin Richie
Photographers: Christine Polomsky, Tim Grondin
Photo Stylist: Jan Nickum

acknowledgments

I have always loved to look at photo albums and reminisce about the great times in my life. My family is always present in those pages of pictures, both the loved ones who are still with us, and those who have passed. My daughter Maria loved to put together scrapbooks, and she created quite a few while she was at college. I feel so blessed that I have these books now since she has passed away. They are a way for me to feel close to her—flipping through the pages and seeing all her hard work and creativity helps me remember her vividly. I will treasure these books always.

I hope you too will find this book helpful in creating memory books of your own that you will be able to share with your children, grandchildren and friends.

dedication

As I worked on creating this book, I had plenty of time to think about what was important to me. Over and over again, images of my family members were my inspiration, and so I would like to dedicate this book to all families. The word family brings a smile to my face and warms my heart, and I hope the same is true for you. Our families stand by us, support us and love us, and we should always embrace them in any way that we can.

As you create the projects in this book, I hope you will find joy in the family memories that you relive. I hope you will also be inspired to make new memories together. After raising seven children, I know how difficult it can be to get everyone together, but I challenge you to put aside one night each week to have dinner and a few laughs with some family members. You could even make some of the projects in this book as a family activity. Pull out those old shoeboxes of pictures and create family bonds that can last forever.

table of contents

introduction

A little over a year ago, my husband and I left the house that all of our children had grown up in and moved into a new home. Although it was difficult to leave behind all of the family memories that we created in that house, we are happy to be living closer to our children, and we're looking forward to creating new memories as our family grows.

Packing up the old and moving into the new, I had the unique opportunity to look both back through the years that had passed and forward into the years to come. I realized that time would eventually deteriorate old Halloween costumes and children's artwork left in boxes, so I started thinking about how I could capture the feelings that picking up an old baseball glove or a well-loved baby doll triggered inside of me.

Right now, many people are preserving their memories in scrapbooks, and my move inspired me to think about what I wanted my own scrapbook to look like. I began to set aside items to include in a personal memory scrapbook, and I started to think of different ways to add my own personal touch to the pages with painting. As more and more ideas rolled around in my head, it dawned on me that painting and papercrafting were natural partners. I began to think about ways to incorporate aspects of painting into papercrafting, and pretty soon I had material for an entire book about making cards, gifts and gift wrap and, yes, scrapbook pages with painted detail.

Personalized cards, homemade gifts and gift wrap and scrapbook pages devoted to loved ones are all great ways to preserve memories in a lasting format. Creating all of the unique projects in this book will also let your individual personality shine through because each project is different depending on who makes it. In this book, I've included ideas that everyone—including painters, crafters and scrapbook enthusiasts—can use to put their personal stamps on the artwork they make to preserve their most cherished memories. Each section in this book combines painting and papercrafting to inspire you to "get outside of the box" and explore different ways to capture each of life's special moments.

BASIC materials

With the recent upsurge in scrapbooking, you'll find that shopping for supplies is just as much fun as creating the projects themselves. An increased demand for specialty papercrafting materials and tools means that new inventions seem to hit the market daily, making even some of the more mundane tasks fun. Take advantage of the abundance of papers, paints, brushes, embellishments, ephemera and tools available—just walking down the aisle of a craft store will give you lots of fabulous ideas for your next project. While it might be tempting, there is no need to buy every tool that is currently on the market—if you did you wouldn't have any room to work! However, you should have some basic painting and papercrafting supplies. After you have stocked up on the most basic supplies, you can start to expand your crafter's closet with some of the other innovative tools and materials that will give your projects a special, personalized touch. As your expertise grows, I'm sure you'll want to try out as many of the new products available as possible.

There are many different types of projects in this book, but all of them use the same basic materials and tools. You'll need a selection of paints, brushes and papers as well as some specialty tools. While all of these materials come in different styles, I've recommended the kinds of paints and brushes that work best for papercrafting projects. All of these supplies are easily found at your local craft, scrapbooking and rubber-stamping stores.

PAPERCRAFTING supplies

It's an exciting time for papercrafting because of all the great new materials and tools now available. Just a few years ago, the only decorative-edge scissors available were pinking shears. Now there are scissors to cut just about any border imaginable. And decorative-edge scissors aren't the only hot new things on the market—I remember about five years ago a simple heart-shaped paper punch was impossible to find, no matter how many craft stores I searched. I finally found one at a teacher's supply store. Today paper punches in a multitude of shapes are available everywhere stationery is sold.

In this book, we will be creating art on paper backgrounds in various ways, using a wide array of techniques and mediums, including ink, paint, decorative chalk and colored pencils. You'll learn how to use stamps to create sophisticated designs by coupling them with techniques like heat embossing, as well as how to spice up stamped images with colored pencils and decorative chalks. In addition, many of the projects layer papers in interesting ways to create original borders in every color combination imaginable. You'll see how easy it is to combine different aspects of papercrafting and painting to create unique cards, gifts and gift wrap, and scrapbook pages.

PAPER & other embellishments

Because this book combines aspects of painting and papercrafting, we will be using all types of paper—from gift bags to napkins to vellum and artist's watercolor paper. With the rise in popularity of scrapbooking, there is an abundance of colors, styles and textures of paper available. Even cardstock and vellum come in patterns and different colors. The papers that I use in this book are merely a suggestion of surface type. Feel free to take the designs to any type or color of paper. Since the paper selection is so varied, choosing a color and design that suit your purpose and personality is a wonderful way to add your signature to any project. Along with the scrapbook boom have come endless choices for embellishments—from stickers and charms to eyelets and brads in an array of colors and shapes. Add special finishing touches to any project with the embellishments you choose.

PAPER

TEXT PAPER (1): Text-weight paper is a medium-weight paper available in many colors, patterns, textures and finishes. Thanks to the popularity of scrapbooking, text paper has patterns ranging from chocolate frosting to fleur-de-lis and everything in between.

VELLUM (2): Vellum, sometimes called translucent paper, is characterized by its see-through quality. It can be found in many colors and designs and is available in both text-weight and cardstock weight. Text-weight vellum works well as an overlay on patterned papers. You can print text on a piece of vellum and then secure it on top of cardstock. Any pattern or design on the cardstock would be visible, though muted, through the vellum.

CARDSTOCK (3): Cardstock, often referred to as cover stock, is a heavier-weight paper. Available in many colors, patterns, textures and finishes, ranging from smooth to heavily textured and matte to glossy, cardstock works well as a base for a card. Blank cardstock is available in reams that can be used in your computer printer.

ARTIST'S WATERCOLOR PAPER: Watercolor paper is a fine paper that comes in different weights and finishes made especially for use with watercolors. For transparent watercolors, most artists prefer a rough or cold-press finish. A smoother finish, such as hot press, is desirable for opaque watercolors, printmaking and drawing.

EMBELLISHMENTS

EYELETS (4): Small metal cylinders that come in many different shapes and colors, eyelets are used to hold layers of paper together and also simply for decoration. Use a small hammer and an eyelet setting head to secure them.

CHARMS (5): Charms in all sizes, shapes and materials are very popular in papercrafting. Tie them on with a ribbon or tack them on with a brad to add a final touch.

RIBBONS (6): Ribbons come in all colors and widths and are great for adding borders and bows to cards, scrapbook pages and gift wrap.

BRADS: Brads are functional and decorative elements that can be used to hold layers of paper together. They are made of many different materials and come in a variety of colors and shapes. Brads have a decorative head that shows on the front side of your project, and two prongs in back that poke through the paper and are flattened on the back side to hold the brad in place and also to secure any layers of paper.

ADHESIVES & OTHER papercrafting supplies

Adhesive doesn't just mean glue or paste anymore. There are many kinds of adhesives available, from permanent to re-positionable. In addition, every papercrafter needs a quality pair of handheld scissors, a selection of paper punches and a reliable ruler. You probably already have most of these supplies, so make sure to have them on hand as you begin.

ADHESIVES AND CUTTING & MEASURING TOOLS

STICKER MACHINE (1): This "machine" can turn any piece of paper into a sticker. Xyron is the most popular brand and comes in sizes that make stickers from about 1" (3cm) wide to full-page stickers. To use it, simply wind the handle and out pops your picture, sandwiched between clear cellophane and an opaque backing. Peel off the backing and the cellophane and voilà—your artwork has become a sticker. The Xyron also has cartridges for cold laminating.

RULERS (2): Even rulers are not straight any more. Now there are decorative "straight" edges that you can place on the paper to tear the paper against, creating a quick and relaxed decorative edge. Why do I call it a "relaxed decorative edge"? While cutting paper with decorative-edge scissors creates a precise cut where everything is uniform and structured, tearing paper against a decorative-edge ruler allows the fibers in the paper to take control, resulting in an uneven edge. This less-than-perfect edge gives a more casual feeling, perfect for a card inviting a friend to lunch.

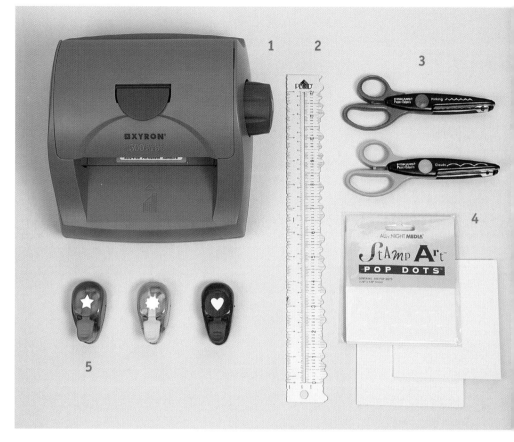

SCISSORS (3): There are plenty of decorative scissors available to match each and every kind of decorating personality. But don't throw away your straight-edge scissors yet; you will still use them. Put the decorative-edge scissors on your wish list or reward yourself monthly with a new pair.

DIMENSIONAL ADHESIVE (4): "Pop dots" are adhesives that lift the attached object off of the background surface. They are available in a variety of thicknesses and can be stacked to make them thicker. They

are made of a thick soft foam that collapses when pressed and springs up when the pressure is off, so no matter how many you use in a scrapbook it will remain closed and the page will spring to life when opened.

PAPER PUNCHES (5): Paper punches come in all shapes and sizes. Purchase the punches as needed. Some of the better-made punches can be fairly expensive and will last a lifetime.

DOUBLE-SIDED ADHESIVE: If you want to archive your work, you need to use acid-free double-sided tape. Again, it is available in permanent and re-positionable.

PAINTING supplies

In this book I use FolkArt Papier Paints and the FolkArt One Stroke brushes that are specifically made for use with Papier Paints. The paints are available in a wide array of colors and finishes, and the brushes come in a range of shapes and sizes that will make painting a breeze. The stiffer bristles of the FolkArt One Stroke brushes are necessary for spreading the paints, which have no water in them. The bristles are still flexible and have the nice spring that is necessary for using the One Stroke Painting Technique, and their softer tips minimize brush lines. There are several kinds of brushes available, and you'll be using a few different types to make the projects in this book.

PAINTS

FOLKART PAPIER PAINTS: Acid-free and archival-safe, these paints are made especially for use on paper, but they can be used on any surface that is not exposed to water or heat. Once cured, these non-blocking paints won't stick to other paper surfaces and won't crack if the paper is bent. The low water content and quick-drying property of these paints result in minimal warping of the paper. In addition, FolkArt Papier Paints provide a beautiful non-flattening dimensional effect when cured. Papier Paints can be used with brushes to fill in large areas, and they can also be used with an applicator tip to create letters and other detail work.

FLOW MEDIUM: Developed for use with the Papier Paints, this medium allows the paint to flow more smoothly when applied with a brush. Although it appears cloudy when it comes out of the bottle, it dries to a crystal-clear finish, making it perfect for achieving floating effects. Load the brush with a little paint, dip the chiseled edge into a puddle of Flow Medium and then add more paint to the brush until it is fully loaded. Too much Flow Medium on the brush will result in the paint becoming transparent when dry, which does make for a very nice effect when desired.

BRUSHES

SCRIPT LINER (1): The long bristles of this brush hold a generous amount of paint. Use it to paint small details and long, thin objects.

SCRUFFY BRUSH (2): These paintbrushes have a fan-like flare and are used for painting mosses, wisteria, lilacs, certain hair and fur, and for creating shading textures. They are not used with water.

FLAT BRUSHES (3): A paintbrush with a flat, even edge that is generally used to paint any object that has a straight edge. Flat brushes come in different sizes, ranging from no. 2 (smallest) to no. 16 (largest).

ROUND BRUSH: A brush that is made up of bristles that come to a point in the center and are gently rounded on the outside. They are generally used to paint any object with a curving edge. Like flat brushes, they come in different no. sizes.

PAINTER'S POINTER

The chisel edge is the straight bottom edge of a flat brush, which is used to start and finish most of the strokes used to paint flowers, leaves and vines in the One Stroke Painting Technique.

TRANSFERRING & OTHER painting supplies

Although I encourage you to paint freehand whenever possible, it is sometimes reassuring to use a pattern. With a few basic supplies, you will be able to transfer any image onto your work surface to take some of the guess work out of painting (see Basic Painting Techniques, page 23). You'll also need a few supplies, including a paint palette and a water basin, to make your painting go smoothly.

TRANSFERRING SUPPLIES

TRANSFER PAPER (1): Transfer paper is used to transfer patterns from tracing paper to the work surface. The preferred transfer paper is graphite paper. This paper has a chalk-like residue on one side that is easily transferred. Even dragging the paper on the surface leaves a residue.

STYLUS (2): A stylus is a tool with a rounded tip on one or both ends that doesn't leave residue on the pattern itself as a pencil would during transfer. A stylus is also used for dry embossing in papercrafting. The stylus shown below has a clip on one end that can be used to hold sponges for stenciling.

STENCILS (3): Use stencils to paint a design onto any surface, including paper. Before applying paint to the open areas in the stencil, make sure that you secure the stencil. As you fill in the open areas with paint, remember that you can always add more color, but you can't always take

it away. Also, never stroke the paintbrush toward the edge of the cutout because it pushes paint under the stencil, making a sloppy edge.

TRACING PAPER (4): Tracing paper is a slightly transparent paper sometimes referred to as onion paper. Trace the pattern onto the tracing paper to preserve the original pattern. Vellum can also be used as tracing paper. Although it is more costly than standard tracing paper, it is thicker, more transparent and more durable.

OTHER PAINTING SUPPLIES

WATER BASIN (5): A good basin will have a raking area used to clean the brushes. Especially when changing from a dark to a light color, get as much paint as possible out of the bristles. By gently raking the bristles along the bottom of the water basin, you are "pulling" the paint out of the bristles. Raking will not harm synthetic bristles as long as you are dragging the bristles across the raking area rather than trying to push them. The other side of a quality water basin will have slots to rest the brush in, keeping the bristles in the water and off of the bottom of the basin. Make sure to keep all used brushes in the water until you can clean them properly.

PAINT PALETTE (6): I use foam plates as my palette because they provide a firm surface for blending and do not absorb the moisture from the paint. I also use my One Stroke palette to hold my plates.

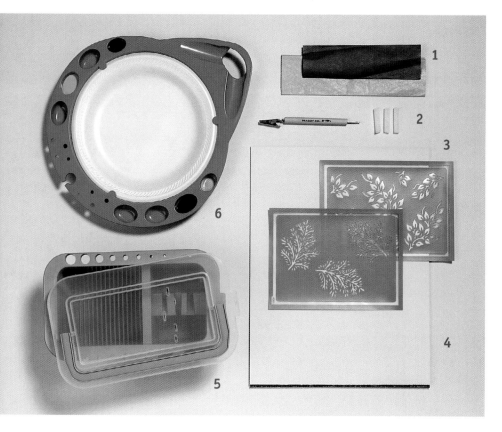

BASIC PAINTING techniques

Teaching people to paint is my passion—I wish I could get everyone to try to paint a little. I really enjoy watching people that I teach "get it." Of course, getting it does take practice. Sometimes we forget what it is like to be a beginner, and we need to be reminded that everything takes time. Babies have to crawl before they walk, and they have to walk before they can run, skip or jump. The same is true for painting. You need to learn how to load and hold your brush first. And you must learn individual strokes before you can put them together. Don't expect to make the perfect stroke right away. But do expect to improve. My roses look better now than they did five years ago, and I thought they looked pretty good back then. Now I look at some of my earlier works and cringe. So don't give up—keep trying. Practice some of these simple techniques, and soon you'll be off and running.

When painting using the One Stroke method, moisten and blot all brushes except for the script liner and the scruffy before loading them with paint.

LOADING THE PALETTE

Although Papier Paints come with an applicator, you can still use them with your brushes. Just squeeze the paints onto your foam plate palette. Shown here are all of the different types of Papier Paint: Opaque (regular paint colors), Mediums and Glitters.

PAINTING WITH applicator tips

Painting lines is easy with the applicator tip that comes with the bottle, especially for medium-weight lines. Screw on a Tip-Pen for an even finer line.

1 TWIST ON TIP-PEN
To use the special Tip-Pen, simply twist on the fine tip. Be sure to rinse this type of tip well when you're done using it.

2 LINE WITH TIP-PEN
The Tip-Pen allows you to pull very fine and intricate lines. This fine control comes in handy for little details like small petals or face details.

DOUBLE LOADING *the brush*

Double loading a paintbrush is a simple technique for creating a multi-colored stroke. In the One Stroke method we double load the brush with contrasting vivid colors to create blending, shading and highlighting all at once. In fact, I use a double-loaded or multi-loaded brush most of the time when I am painting. A properly loaded brush is crucial to painting the One Stroke method, so make sure you follow these steps every time. Moisten the flat brush with Flow Medium prior to loading it with Papier paint.

1 DIP ONE CORNER OF BRUSH INTO PAINT
Dip one corner of the brush into the first paint color to form a triangle of color. Make sure the brush is angled when you dip it into the paint.

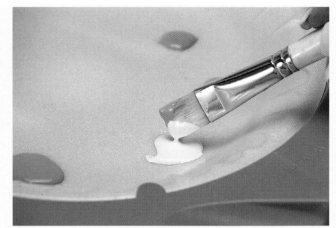

2 DIP OPPOSITE CORNER OF BRUSH INTO PAINT
Dip the other corner of the brush into the second color, forming another triangle.

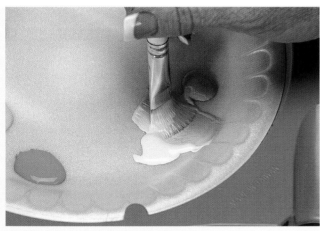

3 WORK PAINT INTO BRISTLES
Place the loaded brush on the palette and stroke it back and forth, pushing down hard against the palette. Stroke the brush over a 2" (5cm) space to work the paint into the bristles.

4 REPEAT STEPS 1–3
Repeat the first three steps until the paint is at least two-thirds up the bristles for a fully loaded brush.

MULTI LOADING the brush

Multi loading takes double loading to the next level and provides even more color and realism to your painting. The added color gives a whole new dimension and more variety to your painting. Don't be afraid to mix colors—some of my best colors were created by accidentally brushing up against another color while I was picking up more paint.

1 DOUBLE LOAD BRUSH
Double load a brush with two colors as shown on page 16. Dip one edge of the brush into a third color, dipping lighter colors to the light side of the brush and darker colors on the dark side of the brush.

2 WORK THIRD COLOR INTO BRISTLES
Firmly stroke the brush back and forth on the foam palette to work the third color into the bristles.

SIDE LOADING the brush

Side load a brush that is smaller than a no. 12 flat. This technique gives you better control of the amount of color on the brush. Side loading is also used when floating a color to add shading.

SIDE LOAD BRUSH
Load the brush with one color of paint. Touch one edge of the brush lightly into the second color. Stroke the brush back and forth on the palette to blend the colors on the brush.

DOUBLE LOADING the scruffy

Do not moisten this brush prior to loading—it needs to be dry to create a textured appearance.

POUNCE EACH SIDE OF SCRUFFY BRUSH INTO PAINT
Pounce one side of the brush into the first paint color. Pounce the other side of the brush into the second color to load the scruffy brush.

LOADING THE script liner

The bristles of a script liner are long and thin, making it easy to paint thin, flowing lines or fine detail work. To use this brush, the paint should be an ink-like consistency so that it flows down to the tips of the bristles. When using the Papier Paints, use Flow Medium to thin the paint, not water.

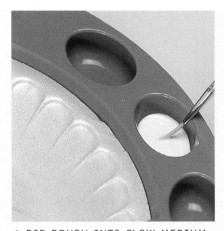

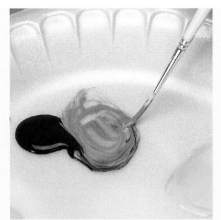

1 DIP BRUSH INTO FLOW MEDIUM
Dip the no. 2 script liner into the Flow Medium on your palette.

2 CREATE AN INKY CONSISTENCY
Make circular motions on the palette at the edge of the paint color to create a paint with an inky consistency.

3 ROLL BRUSH OUT
Roll the brush out of the puddle to test it. If the consistency is right, rolling the brush will make a nice tip on the brush so that it is ready for painting.

LOADING WITH flow medium

Flow Medium is used to help your brush glide along the surface in a smooth, flowing motion. Add it when your brush drags on the surface, which happens often when painting on paper.

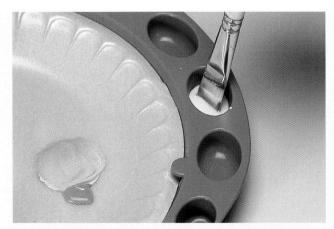

1 DIP BRUSH INTO FLOW MEDIUM
Dip your loaded brush into the Flow Medium.

2 WORK FLOW MEDIUM INTO BRISTLES
Stroke the brush back and forth on the palette to work the Flow Medium into the bristles.

PAINTING a vine

I often use vines and stems in my paintings because they add flow and graceful curves to the designs. Vines help to develop the shape of a design and allow you to see where leaves and flowers should be added. Use very little pressure on the bristles to keep the vine thin, and use more pressure to make the stroke thicker when creating a branch.

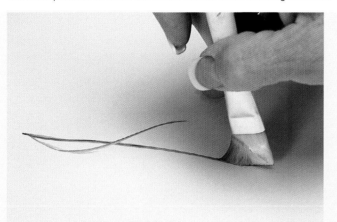

LIFT AND DRAG
With the brush on the chisel edge, touch and tilt back, leading with the lighter color, and then lift and drag the dark bristles.

PAINTING a one-stroke leaf

I use the one-stroke leaf to fill and finish a design. It can also create a slight turn to draw the eye to another area of the design without detracting from the overall appearance. Start with a few leaves and add more as necessary.

1 TOUCH DOWN
Touch with the bristles and push down onto the surface.

2 TURN
Turn the brush slightly.

3 SLIDE TO LEAF TIP
Slide to the chisel edge of the brush to complete the tip.

4 PULL A STEM
To finish the leaf, pull a stem from the vine about halfway into the leaf, leading with the light color.

PAINTING A *heart leaf*

If you can master this leaf, you can paint any of my leaves. I use this leaf quite often—it is usually the second element that is painted after the vine or branch.

1 MAKE A "V"
With the chisel edge of a brush double loaded with yellow and green, tap twice on the paper to paint a "V." Place the brush down and slide a bit to smooth the start of the stroke.

2 KEEP YELLOW EDGE PIVOTING
Wiggle out and in, keeping the yellow edge pivoted in the middle, with the outer edge forming a fan.

3 SLIDE TO TIP OF LEAF
Slide to the chisel edge to complete the tip.

4 REPEAT FOR OTHER SIDE OF LEAF
Repeat this stroke on the other side, starting on the other side of the "V," to form the leaf.

PAINTING A smooth leaf

At first, most people can paint the first half of the heart leaf and they have trouble painting the second half. I developed this alternative to painting the second half of the leaf, and now I use this stroke to paint most of my leaves.

1 PUSH DOWN AND SLIDE
To paint a smooth leaf, starting at the "V," push down and slide to the tip.

2 REPEAT FOR OTHER SIDE OF LEAF
Repeat this stroke on the other side to complete the leaf.

PAINTING A long, skinny leaf

This leaf also came about by accident. I have found that most people, when they are first learning the one-stroke leaf, can learn to paint this one more easily. Now I use this easy technique in many of my projects.

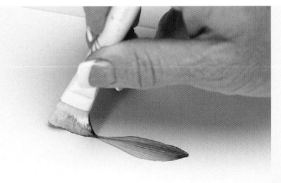

1 TOUCH CHISEL EDGE DOWN
Touch the chisel edge down, and push along the chisel in the direction you're headed.

2 LIFT TO TIP OF LEAF
Slide on the chisel as you lift pressure to the tip of the leaf.

PAINTING daisies

The stroke used to create the daisy is very versatile. You can change the whole look of the flower by using more or less pressure or by pulling the strokes longer or shorter. Experiment with different pressures and lengths, and then try different color combinations. Try Wicker White and Berry Wine, leading first with the Wicker White, and then flip the brush to lead with the Berry Wine—using the same colors in a new way can create a completely different look. The daisy is usually the first flower I teach, mainly because it is so easy but also because it is so versatile.

1 BEGIN TO STROKE FIRST PETAL
Touch the brush to the surface, lean on the chisel toward the center (in the direction you're headed), and pull.

2 PAINT FIRST FOUR PETALS
Continue to paint petals in a circle beginning with 12, 3, 6 and 9 on the clock.

3 FILL IN BETWEEN PETALS
Fill in between these petals to make a complete circle of petals.

4 ADD A SECOND LAYER OF PETALS
To make a fuller daisy, add a second layer of petals in between the first layer.

PAINTING A teardrop shape

The teardrop shape is a versatile intermediate stroke. Remember to let the bristles do the work when painting this shape. The brush should barely move, allowing the bristles to make the stroke.

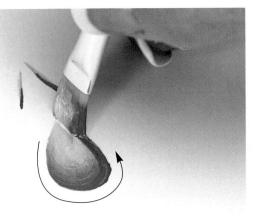

MAKING A TEARDROP
Tap a small inverted "V" onto the surface. Place the chisel edge on one line. Slide down from the first line. Slide up to the second line.

PAINTING A flower shell stroke

Creating this shape, as with the heart leaf, requires a more advanced stroke that can be used to paint all kinds of flowers and leaves.

MAKING A FLOWER SHELL STROKE
Tap the brush twice on the chisel to make two slanted lines. Lay the bristles down on one of the lines and wiggle out and in as you pivot the brush and pull toward the second line.

TRANSFERRING patterns

This book contains some patterns that you can transfer to your surface for painting. However, I encourage you to try to freehand your own design whenever you feel comfortable doing so.

Transfer your pattern onto the surface using graphite paper (gray for a light surface, white for a dark surface) and a stylus or pencil. Insert the graphite paper, dark side down, under the pattern. Trace the pattern onto the surface. Don't trace the curlicues; it's easier to paint these freehand than to try to follow a pattern.

CARDS
& more

with a simple card, you can tell a loved one so much with only a few words. A handmade card created with love and care means more to the recipient than a card that is purchased at a store, and it is more likely to be saved as a memento—the recipient might even add it to his or her scrapbook. Making a card from scratch allows you to personalize it so that it fits the person who receives it. For instance, find out the recipient's favorite flower and then paint that flower on a birthday card. Or maybe you are planning a baby shower or a bridal shower. The guest of honor will feel truly loved and appreciated knowing that the invitations were custom made. And they will be even more flattered when they see that all of the party accessories were also handmade just for them.

As the saying goes, "A picture is worth a thousand words," and taking the time to make something special for someone is priceless. In this section, you'll find an abundance of ideas for celebrating your loved ones' most significant moments. There are birthday and holiday cards, invitations and announcements, and even a get well card. (Who wouldn't be cheered up by the colorful caterpillar who brings wishes of healing with his googly eyes in the Get Well Caterpillar Card on page 36?) Of course, there doesn't have to be a special occasion for you to make and send a thoughtful card. Any day is a good day to send someone you love a "Just-a-Note" Card (page 52) or a greeting bearing a friendly flower, like the Pretty Pansy Card (page 60). Jump right in to cardmaking, and you'll always have a way to show your family and friends that you care.

BUTTERFLY PARTY invitation

Bring the feel of spring to a child's party by decorating invitations, paper plates and party favors with a butterfly motif. All children love to chase after colorful butterflies, and they'll love attending a party that plays on the whimsical beauty of those playful creatures.

What You Will Need

5" × 7" (13cm × 18cm) folded deckle-edge white card

white envelope to fit card

Patchwork Quilt scrapbook paper

no. 16 flat Papier brush

Flow Medium

Tip-Pen applicator for smaller letters, optional

blow dryer

scissors

glue stick

pencil

FOLKART PAPIER COLORS

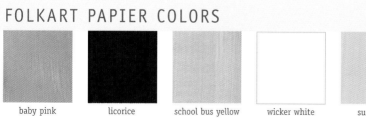

baby pink licorice school bus yellow wicker white sunflower

This pattern appears here at full size.

another gift idea

Theme parties aren't just for kids—create matching place settings and gift bags with a flower motif for a wedding shower, or use baby ducks or fish for a baby shower.

1 CREATE TOP WINGS

With a pencil, sketch the wording on the front of the invitation. Double load the no. 16 flat brush with Wicker White and School Bus Yellow. Touch the brush to the surface of the paper, push the bristles out, and then slide the brush back toward the tip. Make two larger circles for the top wings.

2 ADD LOWER WINGS

Repeat to make two smaller circles for the bottom. Allow the wings to dry, using a blow dryer to speed the process.

3 CREATE WORDING

With Licorice, outline the letters, then add a dot of paint to the ends of each letter. To help keep your lettering and outlines narrow, you may use a narrower tip (such as a Tip-Pen that twists on) that can be purchased separately from the paint.

4 OUTLINE BUTTERFLY
Using Licorice, outline the butterfly. Pull a wavy line for the center of the body.

5 PULL ANTENNAE
Pull the antennae, laying the Licorice bottle on its side and pushing the tip against the paper to get a thin line.

6 CUT OUT SQUARES
Cut out a grouping of four squares from the scrapbook paper. Make sure the butterfly square is included.

7 APPLY GLUE STICK TO SQUARE
Use a glue stick to place glue on the back of the paper.

8 ADHERE SQUARE TO CARD
Adhere the paper square to the card. Cut another square and adhere it to the upper left corner of the envelope.

BUTTERFLY PARTY place setting

Now that the invitations are sent, here are some ideas for carrying the butterfly party theme even further. Consider using one or all of these ideas for complementary butterfly place settings, tablecloth and party favors that will please all your partygoers.

What You Will Need

GENERAL SUPPLIES: glue stick, Tip-Pen for details and small letters, no. 16 flat Papier brush, Flow Medium, pencil, white napkins and white plastic silverware

FOR PLACEMAT: bristol board (11" x 14" [28cm x 36cm]), Patchwork Quilt Scrapbook paper

FOR PLATE: yellow paper plates

FOR CUP: white paper cups

FOR GIFT BAG: gift tissue in pastel colors, small white gift bags, round pink gift tags, ¼" (6mm) pink sheer ribbon, ⅝" (16mm) pink satin ribbon

FOR TABLECLOTH: white tissue tablecloth, stencil roller, squares stencil

PATCHWORK placemat

1 ADHERE ROWS OF SQUARES, SKETCH BUTTERFLIES
Cut out two two-row strips of squares from the scrapbook paper, making each strip 11" (28cm) long. Use a glue stick to attach the strips to each end of the bristol board. Lay a plate in the center of the placemat, then use a pencil to sketch in butterflies on the placemat. (The plate allows you to see where the butterflies will be visible once the table is set.)

2 PAINT BUTTERFLIES
Double load the no. 16 flat with School Bus Yellow and Wicker White. Paint butterflies on the placemat as shown in steps one and two for the invitation. To make a sideways butterfly, hold the yellow to the outside edge and paint the top wing, using pressure to make a bigger circle. Make the bottom wing using lighter pressure, and overlap the top wing. Use Licorice to outline the wings, and create the bodies using a Tip-Pen.

PRETTY-ENOUGH-TO-EAT plate

1 PAINT BUTTERFLY BORDER
Paint butterflies on the plate, using only Wicker White on the no. 16 flat. Paint one full butterfly and three side-view butterflies. Outline the details with Licorice, using a Tip-Pen.

2 COMPLETE BUTTERFLY DETAILS
Repeat the outlines and details on all of the butterflies. It's OK to hit and miss with the outlining—that just adds to the interest and fun.

QUILTED cup

BUTTERFLY bag

NAPKIN ring

ADHERE SQUARE, ADD STITCHES
Cut one square from the scrapbook paper. Spread glue stick on the back and adhere it to the cup. Paint stitching lines on the cup using the Licorice paint and Tip-Pen.

ADD BUTTERFLIES TO BAG & TAG
Paint a side-view butterfly on the favor bag and the gift tag using Wicker White and Sunflower. Detail the butterflies with Licorice. Write the name of one guest on each tag and bag using the Licorice paint and Tip-Pen. Add gift tissue to the bag.

CREATE NAPKIN RING
Cut a pink ribbon to a length of 10"–12" (25cm–30cm). Fold the ribbon in half, push the loop through the hole in the tag and bring the ends of the ribbon through the loop. Pull tight to secure. Fold the corners of the napkin in toward each other to form a pouch. Tie the ribbon around the napkin. Then slip the utensils into the napkin.

BUTTERFLY party tablecloth

1 LOAD ROLLER

Use a roller to paint the tablecloth because a brush will tear it. Simply place a puddle of Baby Pink on the palette and load the roller by running it back and forth through the paint on the palette.

2 STENCIL TABLECLOTH

Place the square stencil onto the tablecloth. Roll the pink paint through the stencil onto the tablecloth.

3 EMBELLISH SQUARES

Clean the stencil and roller. Paint more squares on the tablecloth with a mixture of Wicker White and School Bus Yellow. Embellish the squares on the tablecloth, mimicking the squares on the scrapbook paper. Use Wicker White and the tip to add dots to a pink square.

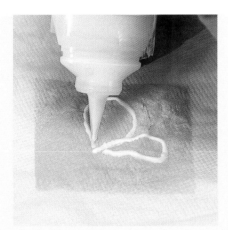

4 CREATE BUTTERFLY

Outline a butterfly on one of the yellow squares with Wicker White.

5 CREATE PINK SWIRL

Paint a Baby Pink swirl on a yellow square, beginning from the outside and spiraling into the center.

6 ADD STITCHES AND BUTTERFLIES

Paint butterflies in between the squares, as shown in steps one and two for the invitation. Make stitching marks around each square with Licorice. Then finish the white butterfly with Licorice details for the body and antennae.

BABY BOY birth announcement

You'll be fishing for compliments when you send out this bubbly announcement for a brand-new baby boy. The brightly colored fish and embellished details will leave no doubt that you're proud of the recent addition to your family (or make it for a friend!).

What You Will Need

olive green linen folded card, 5" × 7" (13cm × 18cm)

blue plaid scrapbook paper (Daisy D's)

white cardstock

announcement from vellum book (or printed on vellum)

no. 8 flat Papier brush

no. 16 flat Papier brush

Flow Medium

¼" (6mm) sapphire metallic square gems

⅛" (3mm) blue square eyelets, 4

green braided self-adhesive yarn, for name

googly eye

small adhesive dots

mini pop dots

deckle-edge ruler

³⁄₃₂" (1mm) hole punch (Creative Impressions)

eyelet-setting tool

hammer

scissors

cutting mat

glue stick

double-sided tape

pencil

FOLKART PAPIER COLORS

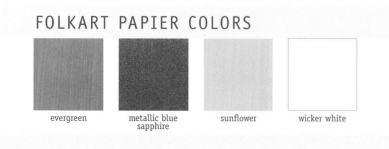

evergreen   metallic blue sapphire   sunflower   wicker white

This pattern appears here at full size.

PAINTER'S POINTER

If you plan on using a plaid paper that is in different colors than the one I used, pick out paint colors that coordinate.

1 BASECOAT FISH AND PAINT GILL

Cut the plaid paper to 4½" × 3½" (11cm × 9cm). Basecoat the fish body with solid Evergreen using the no. 16 flat brush. Side load Sunflower onto the no. 8 flat brush and paint highlights around the fish. Paint on the gill.

2 ADD DAISY STROKES TO FINS AND LIPS

Double load the no. 8 flat brush with Sunflower and Evergreen. Paint small daisy strokes (see Basic Painting Techniques, page 22) for the lips, the fins at the bottom of the fish and the fins at the top. Turn the paper as needed to pull the strokes.

3 EMBELLISH FISH WITH SUNFLOWER

Embellish the fish with Sunflower, making more gills and dots and lines on the tail.

4 ADD GOOGLY EYE AND BUBBLES

Attach the eye with a small adhesive dot. Paint the bubbles with Metallic Blue Sapphire using the tip of the bottle, making the bubbles smaller as they go up. Highlight the bubbles with a dot of Wicker White.

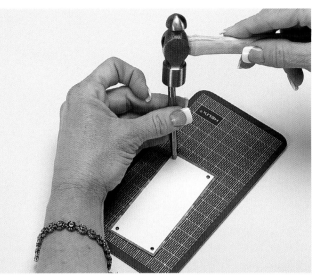

5 PUNCH HOLES IN CORNERS OF LAYERED RECTANGLE

Cut a piece of plaid paper to 4⅛" × 1⅞" (10cm × 5cm). Cut a piece of white cardstock to 4" × 1¾" (10cm × 4cm). Center the white onto the plaid and lightly glue in place. Allow glue to dry. Set the layered rectangle face up on a cutting mat and punch a hole in each corner using the hole punch and hammer.

6 SPELL "BOY" WITH YARN

Pencil the word "BOY" onto the small piece of white cardstock. Cover the letters with the self-adhesive yarn, placing large pieces on each section and then cutting them to the right size.

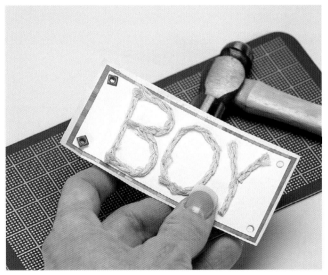

7 SET EYELETS

Place the eyelets through the holes, and then set them on the back with the setting tool and hammer.

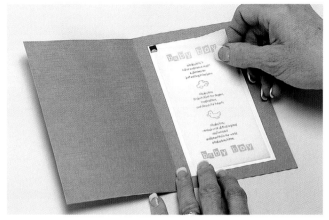

8 ATTACH VELLUM PRINTED WITH ANNOUNCEMENT

For the inside of the card, cut a piece of white cardstock to 3¼"
× 6" (8cm × 15cm). Adhere it to the inside of the card. Place a
mini pop dot on the back of a metallic square gem. Attach the
vellum to the white cardstock using the pop dot, making sure to
center the vellum announcement over the white cardstock.

CRAFTER'S TIP

Print your own announcement on vellum or purchase preprinted
vellum and include a separate note with your baby's information.

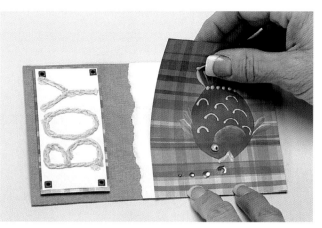

9 ASSEMBLE CARD FRONT

To assemble the front of the card, affix the "BOY" rectangle with
mini pop dots. Cut another piece of white cardstock to 4½" ×
4½" (11cm × 11cm). Using the deckle-edge ruler, tear the edge
off of one side of the paper, removing about ½" (12mm) of
paper. Tape this piece to the bottom of the card, then tape the
plaid fish piece over it using double-sided tape.

BABY GIRL birth announcement

Create a softer look for an "It's a Girl" birth announcement
by using pastel colors and a dusting of glitter. A banner
attached with pop dots gives the card a festive look.

1   Cut out a banner shape from cardstock or bristol board.
    Use stickers to spell out "It's a Girl."

2   Tint the edges of the banner and the card with pink chalk.

3   Load the no. 8 flat with Baby Pink and paint the rattle's
    handle and around the outer shape of the rattle.

4   Load the no. 8 flat with School Bus Yellow and paint the
    bow around the handle of the rattle.

5   Outline the bow with Pearl White Metallic.

6   Paint little hearts around the rattle's head and handle with
    Calypso Sky, Fresh Foliage and School Bus Yellow.

7   Fold the banner and adhere it to the top of the card with
    pop dots. Tie a multi-colored ribbon around the spine of
    the card as a finishing touch.

GET WELL CATERPILLAR card

This card is designed with a child in mind, but anyone under the weather will be cheered up by this silly caterpillar whose head pops up from the front of the card.

What You Will Need

4¼" × 5¾" (11cm × 15cm) white folded card

bristol board

⅛-inch (3mm) mini scruffy brush

¾-inch (19mm) enamel scruffy brush

cosmetic sponge

blending chalks

letter stickers to spell "Get Well Soon"

green braided self-adhesive yarn

small googly eyes

stylus

squares stencil

small adhesive dots

brass letter stencil (All Night Media)

light box, optional

small scissors

fine-point permanent marker

pencil

FOLKART PAPIER COLORS

fresh foliage

school bus yellow

wicker white

IT REALLY BUGS ME

WHEN YOU'RE SICK

Enlarge this pattern to 125% to bring to full size.

another gift idea

This cheerful caterpillar works well for a card of encouragement, especially if you add a painted butterfly on the inside of the card. Sometimes your loved ones need a reminder of the wonderful transformations that occur as a result of troubled times.

PAINTER'S POINTER
After removing the scruffy brush from its packaging, make sure to "fluff the scruff" before using the brush. Gently pull on the bristles and then twist them in the palm of your hand to form them into their natural oval shape.

1 POUNCE CATERPILLAR ONTO BRISTOL BOARD
Pencil a 2½" × 2½" (6cm × 6cm) square in the center of a white piece of bristol board. Begin with the mini scruffy brush and pounce circles with Wicker White and School Bus Yellow on one side and Fresh Foliage on the other side of each circle. Begin with a circle about 1" (2cm) in diameter, and continue making smaller and smaller circles until the caterpillar's body is formed.

2 CREATE CATERPILLAR HEAD
On a separate scrap of bristol board, create another single large circle for the head of the caterpillar. This will be cut out later on.

3 RULE LINES FOR WORDING
Rule lines for the words "It Really Bugs Me" along the top left inside of the card. Rule lines for the words "When You're Sick" at the bottom left inside of the card. Make your lines light so you can erase them later.

4 BEGIN STENCILING LETTERS
Mark the center of the line with a dot to help you stencil the words from the center out. Place the stencil face down (the letters will be backward) on a light box or tape it to a window that is getting lots of light. Place the card on top of the stencil with the lined side up, aligning the mark you made for the center with the center letter. Trace the letters with the stylus.

5 STENCIL SQUARE
Continue tracing the letters, working your way out from the center. Repeat for the wording on the bottom line. With a pencil and the square template, draw a 2½" (6cm) square, centering it between the words on the card front.

6 CUT OUT SQUARE
Use a small pair of scissors to cut out the square. Erase any visible pencil lines.

7 CHALK FRONT OF CARD
Open the card flat on a scrap piece of paper with the front facing up. Use the large scruffy brush to rub yellow chalk onto the front of the card.

8 RUB CHALK OVER RAISED LETTERING
Use a cosmetic sponge to rub red chalk over the raised lettering. Use just a bit of chalk and soften as you go.

9 BLEND CHALK COLORS

Add a bit of green to the yellow with the large scruffy brush to bring out the green in the caterpillar. Soften the red chalk with yellow chalk using the large scruffy.

10 CUT OUT CATERPILLAR

Use small scissors to carefully cut out the caterpillar. Cut the head out as well.

11 ADD LETTER STICKERS INSIDE

Place the letter stickers on the inside of the card to spell "Get Well Soon." Begin with the "E" in "Well" to determine a center point.

12 ADHERE BODY AND HEAD

Adhere googly eyes to the caterpillar head. Draw a mouth on the caterpillar with a fine-tip permanent marker. Put a pop dot on the back of each segment of the caterpillar body. Close the card and place the caterpillar in the center of the square. Place a pop dot on the back of the head and place it on top of the end segment of the body.

13 ADD TRIM TO WINDOW

Carefully place the self-adhesive green braided yarn around the square opening of the card. Trim away the excess yarn with sharp scissors to finish border.

CRAFTER'S TIP

The large pop dots add more height to a project like this. Cut the dots in half to fit onto the smaller segments of the body.

EASTER greetings

I created this colorful card for my grandchildren because they love coloring Easter eggs so much. The eggs are made by using a double-loaded brush to fill in some simple oval shapes. Once completed, the card is bright and cheery enough for any child, and elegant enough for your most sophisticated friend.

What You Will Need

pink pearlescent scrapbook paper

pink and green plaid scrapbook paper

white cardstock

no. 8 flat Papier brush

Flow Medium

butterfly eyelets

brass letters stencil (All Night Media)

mini pop dots

double-sided tape

light box

stylus

decorative corner punch (Posh Impressions)

eyelet-setting tool

hammer

protective surface

pencil

FOLKART PAPIER COLORS

baby pink   calypso sky   glitter disco   pumpkin   school bus yellow   wicker white

This pattern appears here at full size.

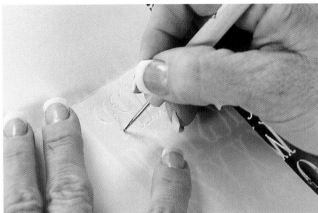

1 STENCIL LETTERS ONTO PINK PAPER

Cut a piece of pink pearlescent scrapbook paper to 10¾" × 6" (27cm × 15cm). Fold the card so that the front is about ¼" (6mm) shorter than the back of the card. To emboss the paper, you'll work on the back side of the front of the card. Draw a pencil line on the back of the paper, near the top of the front, to line up the letters. Place the paper face down on the light box, then line up the letter stencil underneath the paper. Run the stylus over the paper in the grooves of the stencil letters, taking care to press firmly, but not so hard as to tear the paper.

another gift idea

Hatch a brilliant idea by painting a chick emerging from one of these eggs, and you'll have a perfect birth announcement card.

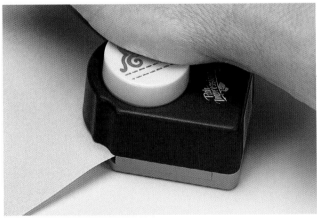

2 PUNCH OUT CORNERS OF CARD

Use the decorative punch to embellish the bottom corners on the front of the card.

3 TAPE DECORATIVE PAPER INSIDE CARD

Cut a piece of coordinated paper to fit the inside of the card. Tape the paper inside the card with double-sided tape.

4 SKETCH EGGS

Cut a piece of white cardstock to 3" × 4" (8cm × 10cm). Punch holes in each of the corners, then sketch in three overlapping eggs with a pencil.

5 PAINT EGGS

Double load the no. 8 flat with Wicker White and whatever color you'd like your eggs to be. I used Calypso Sky, School Bus Yellow and Baby Pink. Start with the lefthand egg, and move to the right. The eggs will be layered over each other, so keep your eyes on the outer edge of the egg, taking care not to paint on top of an overlapping egg.

6 SET BUTTERFLY EYELETS IN CORNERS

Place the butterfly eyelets into the holes, then turn the paper and set the eyelets with the setting tool and hammer.

CRAFTER'S TIP

When setting decorative eyelets like these, take care not to hammer the back too hard or the eyelets will crimp the paper.

7 EMBELLISH EGGS

Adhere the cardstock onto the card with pop dots. To finish, embellish the eggs with zigzag lines and dots using Pumpkin, Calypso Sky, Baby Pink and Glitter Disco.

HALLOWEEN greetings

Wish your favorite ghouls and goblins a happy Halloween with this spooky dimensional card. The simply constructed metal web stands out well against the black background, and the hauntingly cute ghost bobs around charmingly.

1 Paint the ghost on black cardstock using Wicker White and Flow Medium. Cut out the ghost, and cut holes for the eyes and mouth. Attach the ghost to the card using thin-gauge wire bent into a spring.

2 Paint the jack-o-lantern on white cardstock using School Bus Yellow and Pumpkin. Paint the face using Licorice. Allow to dry, and cut out. Create a handle with black floss and attach the pumpkin to the ghost.

3 Paint the moon using Wicker White and School Bus Yellow. Paint the face using Licorice and Wicker White.

4 Make the web by bending silver wire through holes in the card and gluing in place. Tie silver metallic thread as cross pieces.

5 To make the spider, pounce a round shape on white cardstock using Amethyst and Wicker White. Allow to dry, and cut out the shape. Glue on black wire to make legs and then paint a face on the top. Attach to the web using silver metallic thread.

PEACE on earth

Send your best season's greetings with this cheerful card. The bright red and green color scheme is perfect for sending warm holiday wishes, and the banner with gold sparkly lettering lends the card a festive air.

1 Cut out a banner from cardstock or white bristol board.

2 Write the words "Peace on Earth" on the banner using Antique Gold Glitter.

3 Double load a ½-inch (12mm) scruffy brush with Thicket and Fresh Foliage. Pounce the brush in a circle to make the wreath.

4 Paint the berries with the tip of the bottle of Engine Red.

5 Paint pine needles with the applicator tip of Fresh Foliage.

6 Fold the banner and attach it to the card using pop dots.

STRIPED HYDRANGEA card

I love to paint hydrangeas almost as much as I love to paint roses because they are such delicate flowers, and yet they are hearty as well. Part of their beauty stems from the fact that they are never alone—they grow in clumps of multiple blooms. Show someone that you care and that they will never be alone by giving them a card with a painted hydrangea.

What You Will Need

5" × 7" (13cm × 18cm) pink striped folded card (All Night Media)

glossy wrapping paper in shades of green (or Donna Dewberry Faux Finish wallpaper)

½-inch (12mm) enamel scruffy brush

no. 8 flat Papier brush

no. 16 flat Papier brush

Flow Medium

FolkArt one-stroke leaves stencil

FOLKART PAPIER COLORS

fresh foliage

metallic rose shimmer

sunflower

thicket

wicker white

1 STENCIL LEAF ONTO CARD FRONT

Place the leaf stencil onto the pink cardstock. Pounce Sunflower, Wicker White and Thicket into the stencil openings using the scruffy brush.

2 PAINT FIRST HALF OF LEAF

Multi load Thicket, Fresh Foliage and a little bit of Sunflower onto the no. 16 flat. To paint this leaf, wiggle up one side, then slide the brush to the tip of the leaf.

3 PAINT SECOND HALF OF LEAF

Turn the paper, and start the second side of the leaf at the top again. Instead of wiggling this side, just slide the brush to the tip to create a smooth edge.

4 ADD MORE LEAVES

Paint more leaves, wiggling both sides on some for variety (see Basic Painting Techniques, page 20-21).

5 BEGIN ONE-STROKE LEAVES
Load the no. 8 flat with Fresh Foliage and a little bit of Sunflower. To begin to paint a one-stroke leaf, push the bristles down on the paper (see Basic Painting Techniques, page 19).

6 FINISH ONE-STROKE LEAVES
Turn, slide and lift to finish the one-stroke leaf. Paint several of these leaves in different sizes.

7 CREATE FIVE-PETAL FLOWERS
Double load the no. 8 flat with Metallic Rose Shimmer and Wicker White. To paint five-petal flowers, touch the bristles to the surface, push out and lift the bristles to form a petal.

another gift idea

It can be challenging to find a sympathy card that is appropriately sorrowful and yet also expresses hope for the future. Stamp the words "You're Never Alone" on the front or inside of this card to communicate hope to the recipient.

8 CLUSTER PETALS TOGETHER

Paint five of these petals together to form a flower, slightly overlapping the petals in spots.

9 ADD DAISY STROKES

Add a few daisy strokes to the flower by touching the bristles to the surface, leaning the brush toward the cluster and sliding the brush as you lift (see Basic Painting Techniques, page 22).

10 OUTLINE TRAILING FLOWERS

Loosely outline the trailing flowers with Wicker White using the applicator tip.

PAINTER'S POINTER

The Papier Paint will hold its shape if you allow it to dry for at least 48 hours. If you should place something on top of the paint and it flattens before it dries, apply more paint on top of it and allow it to dry.

11 ADD SUNFLOWER DOTS TO CENTERS
Outline the main cluster of flowers with Wicker White, and then add dots to the center with Sunflower.

12 OUTLINE LEAVES
Add a few strokes to the outside of the arrangement to embellish the leaves.

13 ADD DECORATIVE ACCENTS
Outline the leaves with Fresh Foliage and add some decorative accents along the edges of the leaves and flowers.

HYDRANGEA wrapping paper

1 STENCIL ON FERNS AND PAINT FLOWERS

Cut enough wallpaper or wrapping paper to wrap your package. Place the stencil on the paper. With Sunflower, Wicker White and Thicket on your palette, pounce the scruffy onto the fern stencil. Alternate picking up the three colors and move the stencil around to randomly cover the paper. Paint five-petal flowers (see steps seven and eight of card) on the wrapping paper with the no. 8 flat double loaded with Wicker White and Metallic Rose Shimmer. Then paint some trailing flowers using the same stroke.

2 OUTLINE PETALS

Loosely outline each of the petals with Wicker White using the applicator tip.

3 DOT FLOWER CENTERS WITH SUNFLOWER

Dot the centers of the flowers with Sunflower.

4 ADD FLOWERS AFTER GIFT IS WRAPPED

Once the paper has dried, wrap the gift. Tie the bow on loosely, then determine if you need any more flower clusters. Here, I decided I needed one more cluster of flowers to fill in the top of the box.

LOVELY LILAC birthday card

You don't have to be an artist to make this simple and elegant card. With a few colored pencils, clear dome letters and a little white paint, you'll have a beautiful handmade piece of art in only about half an hour. And your loved one will remember your gift for far longer.

What You Will Need

lilac cardstock

white cardstock

light green text-weight paper

Roses and Lilac stamp (All Night Media)

purple lilac ink pad (All Night Media)

medium gray ink pad (All Night Media)

Wicker White FolkArt Papier acrylic paint

colored pencils

pink pen

centering ruler

double-sided tape

scissors

adhesive pop dots

dome alphabet stickers
(Brenda Walton Treasure)

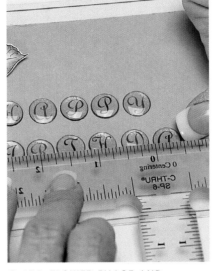

1 STAMP AND COLOR LILAC IMAGE
Ink the lilac stamp with medium gray ink. Stamp the image onto a piece of white cardstock. Color the rose, lilac and leaves in with colored pencils, using lights and darks of each color to achieve depth. Use darker colors around the outside of the shapes and lighter colors on the inside, as shown here on the leaf. Use light pink and dark pink for the rose and light and dark purple and pink on the lilac.

2 ADD FLOWER IMAGE AND LETTERING TO CARD FRONT
Cut a piece of green paper to 5½" × 3½" (14cm × 9cm). Attach the green paper to the card with double-sided tape. Use the pink pen and ruler to draw a border between the edge of the green paper and the edge of the card. Carefully cut out the stamped image. Place pop dots on the back of the cut-out image and place it on the card. Spell out the sentiment with the dome alphabet stickers, taking care to place the middle letters of the sentiment in the center of the card. Use a ruler to keep the letters straight.

3 EMBELLISH WITH WHITE DOTS
Use Wicker White to embellish the card with dots in the corners and all around the green part of the card.

LILAC wrapping paper

Use the same stamp to decorate wrapping paper for a gift. Stamp the flowers in purple ink and use chalk to color them in lightly. You could also color the stamped flowers with colored pencils if you like. Dress it up with a bow, and you'll have a lovely gift package to match your handmade card.

"JUST-A-NOTE" card

While it's easy to make cards for women and girls because of all of the feminine-looking craft supplies, we shouldn't forget that men and boys like to receive cards too. This card is quite simple, but the embossing embellishment techniques make it look impressive. The special man in your life will love it.

What You Will Need

white flecked cardstock

sage green cardstock

black cardstock

metallic gold embossing powder

clear embossing powder

Just a Note rubber stamp (All Night Media)

leaf background stamp (All Night Media)

gold metallic ink pad

Italian Sage pigment ink pad
(All Night Media)

gold leafing pen

⅛" (3mm) gold eyelets, 8

⅜" (10mm) wide variegated sage ribbon

rubber stamp positioner

heat gun

narrow double-sided tape

³⁄₃₂" (1mm) hole punch

eyelet-setting tool

hammer

ruler clamp

protective surface

black fine-tip permanent marker

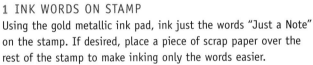

1 INK WORDS ON STAMP

Using the gold metallic ink pad, ink just the words "Just a Note" on the stamp. If desired, place a piece of scrap paper over the rest of the stamp to make inking only the words easier.

another gift idea

Make business better than usual by sending this note to a co-worker or client. The simple, clean lines of this card make it appropriate for a working relationship. Stamp it with "Thank You" and make a few to have on hand in your desk drawer.

2 ALIGN STAMP

Use the stamp positioner to determine where the stamp will end up on the paper in relation to the bar. Stamp the words onto a piece of scrap paper.

3 STAMP WORDS ONTO GREEN CARDSTOCK

Place the small piece of green cardstock over the image you just stamped, then re-ink the stamp and stamp the image onto the green cardstock.

4 SPRINKLE ON GOLD EMBOSSING POWDER

Sprinkle the embossing powder onto the stamped image, making sure to cover all of the ink.

5 MELT POWDER

Tap the excess powder off of the card, and brush away any excess powder with a small dry paintbrush. Pour the excess powder back into the container for use again later. Holding the paper with a clamp, heat the embossing powder with the heat gun until the powder melts.

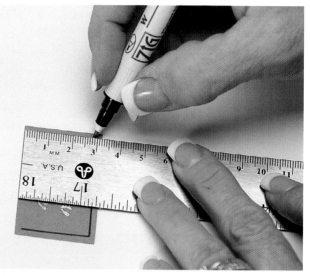

6 CREATE BORDER AROUND STAMPED PHRASE

Draw a narrow border inside the edge of the green paper using a ruler and a fine-tip permanent marker.

7 APPLY GOLD PAINT PEN TO EDGES

Fold the piece of white flecked cardstock in half as the base for your card. Using the gold leafing pen, make a gold border around the folded cardstock by running the pen just along the edge. Cut a piece of black cardstock to 1⅞" × 2½" (5cm × 6cm). Edge the piece of black cardstock in gold with the leafing pen.

8 CREATE LEAF BACKGROUND

Cut another piece of 4¼" × 5½" (11cm × 14cm) white flecked cardstock. Ink the leaf background stamp with sage pigment ink. Stamp the leaves randomly onto the piece of cardstock, being sure to stamp some images off of the edge of the paper.

9 SPRINKLE ON POWDER

Sprinkle clear embossing powder over the sage ink while it's still wet.

10 HEAT POWDER

Tap the excess powder off of the card. Remove any remaining powder that's not stuck to the ink with a small paintbrush. Heat the embossing powder with the heat gun to set it.

11 ADHERE RIBBON

Cut two pieces of ribbon to 4¼" (11cm) and two pieces to 5½" (14cm). Place double-sided tape on the back of each piece of ribbon, then tape them to the stamped cardstock to make a border. Place the two short pieces first, then the longer pieces. Turn the ends under the card and tape them.

12 PUNCH HOLES

Punch holes with the hole punch and hammer in each corner where the ribbon intersects, and set an eyelet in each hole.

13 LAYER COMPLETED PIECES TO FINISH

Set eyelets in each corner of the black cardstock piece. Layer the sentiment onto the piece of black cardstock. Trim a piece of sage cardstock to 3⅝" × 4⅞" (9cm × 12cm). Layer this piece onto the folded base of the card. Layer the ribbon piece onto the sage piece, then layer the black piece onto the ribbon piece.

PURPLE HYDRANGEA card

Hydrangeas are perfect for decorating cards for almost any occasion, and because they come in different colors, you can choose the color that best suits the recipient's taste. This card demonstrates just how versatile the hydrangea is for decorating papercrafts.

What You Will Need

5½" × 8½" (14cm × 22cm) white folded card

white cardstock (for oval)

green scrapbook paper

purple scrapbook paper

⅝" (16mm) wide purple satin ribbon

¼" (3mm) mini scruffy brush

¾" (2cm) brush (for chalks)

ovals stencil

large hydrangea rubber stamp
(All Night Media)

small hydrangea rubber stamp
(All Night Media)

black dye ink pad

lavender pigment ink pad (All Night Media)

blending chalks

colored pencils

gold leafing pen

double-stick tape

large pop dots

mini pop dots

white eraser

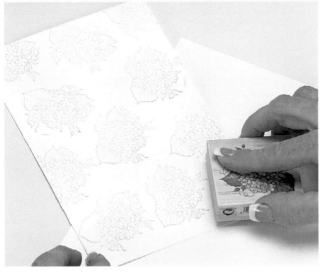

1 CREATE STAMPED BACKGROUND

Stamp the front of the card with the small hydrangea cluster stamp and lavender ink. Stamp the image randomly over the whole front of the card.

another gift idea

Mothers never tire of the handmade gifts given to them by their children. Mom will be proud to display this lovely work of art long after the holiday has passed.

2 STAMP IMAGE ONTO WHITE OVAL

Cut a 3¾" × 4" (10cm × 10cm) oval from white cardstock, an oval 3" × 4½" (8cm × 11cm) from green scrapbook paper and a third oval 3⅜" × 5" (9cm × 13cm) from purple scrapbook paper. Ink the large hydrangea stamp with black ink. To ensure that the image is centered on the oval, turn the stamp inked side up and lay the paper on top of the stamp. Press down on the paper with your hand to make the image. Set the oval pieces aside.

3 BRUSH IN COLOR RANDOMLY

Use chalks and a ¾" (2cm) scruffy to brush in lavender chalk randomly on the front of the card. Add some pink chalk as well.

4 COLOR IN STAMPED HYDRANGEA

Use colored pencils to color in the yellow centers of the hydrangeas. Use bright green chalks on the mini scruffy to color in the centers of the leaves; use pink and lavender and a little green chalk to color in the blossoms. Use dark green colored pencil to color the edges of the leaves, then use the scruffy to soften and mix the green colors on the leaves. By rubbing a soft scruffy over the chalks, you'll blend the colors and soften the look. Use a white eraser to remove any chalk that gets onto the white card.

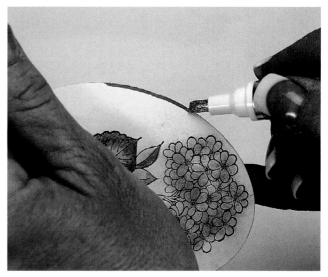

5 APPLY GOLD LEAFING PEN TO EDGES OF OVAL

Use the gold leafing pen to create a border around the white oval and around the edges of the front of the card.

CRAFTER'S TIP

When using paint pens, be sure to reload the paint occasionally by pressing the tip onto a piece of scrap paper.

6 ADD PURPLE RIBBON ONTO SIDES

Cut two pieces of ribbon to 9" (23cm), and place double-sided tape on the back of each piece. Place one ribbon vertically on the fold side of the card, wrapping the excess ribbon around the card and overlapping the ends on the inside of the card. Repeat with the remaining ribbon on the vertical edge. Be sure to place the ribbon to the inside of the gold border.

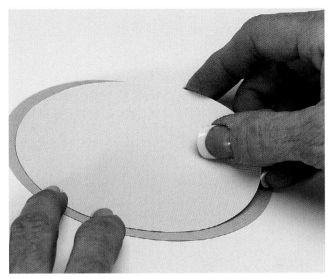

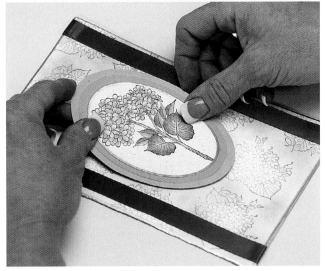

7 LAYER GREEN OVAL

Layer the green oval onto the lavender oval with double-sided tape, making sure to center it so an even border of lavender is visible around the smaller oval.

CRAFTER'S TIP

When using the chalks, be sure to remove the top layer of chalk to expose the softer chalk.

8 LAYER OVALS ONTO CARD

Tape the white oval on top of the green oval, then use large pop dots to secure the layered piece onto the front of the card. Place the oval slightly higher than the center of the card.

9 ADD A BOW TO FINISH

Tie a shoestring bow with 14" (36cm) of purple ribbon, trimming the ends as desired. Adhere the bow to the card with mini pop dots. Use more pop dots to keep parts of the bow flat against the card.

PRETTY PANSY card

I hate searching madly for the perfect paper, and so I often pull colors from my painted image to create my own background paper. You can continue the motif by using the same background on the lining of the card's envelope.

What You Will Need

white folded card

pink swirl-print scrapbook paper

white cardstock (for pansy)

envelope to fit card

no. 8 flat Papier brush

no. 16 flat Papier brush

Flow Medium

decorative fibers

mini glue dots

double-sided tape

Xyron machine, optional

scissors

FOLKART PAPIER COLORS

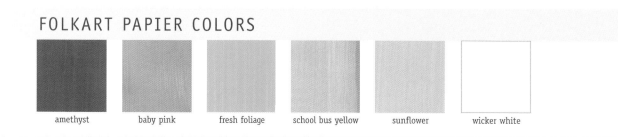

amethyst   baby pink   fresh foliage   school bus yellow   sunflower   wicker white

This pattern appears here at full size.

another gift idea

Pansies are such friendly flowers, so this design is a natural fit to use as an invitation. Simplify the card and make it quicker to make (so you can make multiples) by painting a single pansy, cutting it out and layering it on top of the full sheet of pink paper. Just stamp "You're Invited!" above the pansy, and get the party started right.

1 MAKE A SHELL SHAPE
Double load the no. 16 flat with Baby Pink and Wicker White, then side load School Bus Yellow onto the brush. Make a shell shape on the piece of white card-stock with the yellow toward the inside (see Basic Painting Techniques, page 23).

2 REPEAT PETALS ON EACH SIDE
Pick up more Wicker White and Baby Pink on the brush, then paint side petals on either side of the shell, this time with the pink toward the inside.

3 FINISH PANSY WITH TEARDROPS
On the pink edge of the brush, pick up Amethyst, and pick up School Bus Yellow on the white side. Paint two teardrop strokes with the purple on the outside to finish the pansy (see Basic Painting Techniques, page 23).

4 CREATE PANSY BUDS

Stroke a partial seashell, then stroke two daisy strokes (see Basic Painting Techniques, page 22) on the side to paint the pansy buds using the same purple and yellow double-loaded brush as in step three. Paint two of these pansy buds, one on each side of the full pansy.

5 ADD LEAF CLUSTERS

Double load Sunflower and Fresh Foliage onto the no. 8 flat, occasionally picking up a little School Bus Yellow. Chisel-edge a stem to connect the buds to the pansy (see Basic Painting Techniques, page 19). Paint one-stroke leaves coming off of the stems and around the pansy. Because this cluster will be cut out, be sure to keep the elements nice and close to each other.

6 EMBELLISH PANSIES

Use Wicker White to loosely outline the petals and buds. Embellish the center of the pansy with small strokes of Fresh Foliage and dots of School Bus Yellow.

7 CUT OUT PANSY CLUSTER

Let the paint dry completely. Use small sharp scissors to loosely cut out the cluster, leaving an even white border around the entire painted image. If there's a stray stroke or a leaf you don't like, cut it out.

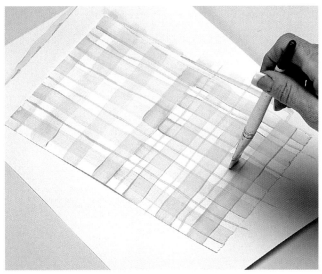

8 PAINT GREEN PLAID LINES FOR OUTSIDE OF CARD

Paint a plaid design on the outside of the card. Start with Fresh Foliage mixed with Flow Medium on the no. 16 flat. Paint lines down the card, reloading the brush when you get to the fold line, if necessary. Use the same color to paint horizontal lines. Don't worry about keeping the lines exactly straight or evenly spaced—do your best and any imperfections will add variety.

9 ADD PINK LINES TO PLAID

Load the no. 16 with Baby Pink and Flow Medium. Use the chisel edge of the brush to paint wiggly pink lines in between each of the green lines. Let dry completely.

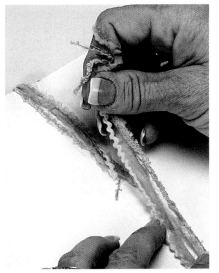

10 ADHERE PINK PAPER, PANSY

Cut a piece of pink scrapbook paper to 6" × 4" (15cm × 10cm). Run it through the Xyron machine or apply double-sided tape to adhere it to the painted card. With a glue stick or mini adhesive dots, glue the cut-out pansies onto the pink paper.

11 ADD DECORATIVE FIBERS

Place a piece of double-sided tape on the front of the card, along the fold. Place a few strands of matching fibers on the front, then wrap the ends onto the inside of the card, using the double-sided tape to adhere them.

12 LINE ENVELOPE

Cut a piece of pink patterned paper to fit the width of the envelope. Line up the paper just below the envelope glue, close the envelope, then tape the paper just below the glue line. Turn the envelope over and cut away any excess paper to the shape of the envelope flap.

GIFTS
& gift wrap

how many times have you gone to wrap a present for someone just to find that you do not have enough wrapping paper? Or, if you do have enough wrapping paper, it is for the wrong type of occasion? I used to have to make a last-minute scramble for adequate paper all of the time. If I needed to wrap a wedding gift, all I seemed to have was children's birthday paper. I finally learned my lesson, and now I just make sure that I have a variety of plain solid-color wrapping paper and gift bags on hand at all times. It's quick and easy to wrap the gift or choose a bag and then embellish it to suit the person receiving it. With the Papier Paints, it's so fun and easy to create handmade motifs that you could make several bags all at once and keep them on hand for any future gift-wrap emergencies.

In this section you'll find creative gift and gift-wrapping ideas for all occasions. There are projects to suit men and women of all ages—from adults to children and "tweens." Each project has a different theme, including palm trees, wedding bells, beads and, of course, flowers. Make the Beach Bag (page 66) to hold a bon voyage gift for that special man in your life. Or you can add a sophisticated spin to any wedding gift by presenting it to the bride and groom in the Silver Wedding Bells Gift Bag (page 70). Mom will love the Roses Gift Wrap (page 78), and the Framed Smiling Flower Faces (page 84) will delight nieces, nephews and grandchildren everywhere. Whatever the occasion and whomever the recipient, this section is sure to have an idea that fits perfectly.

BEACH bag

Finding gift wrap for a man can be a challenge, but this gift bag fits the bill perfectly. The tropical theme of this project works well for a travel send-off and for lots of other occasions. This is a great project for beginners because it uses simple techniques and has only a few steps.

What You Will Need

kraft gift bag

gold gift tag

no. 16 flat Papier brush

Flow Medium

14" (36cm) long decorative fibers in neutral trims plus gold (JoAnn Scrap Essentials)

ruler

pencil

FOLKART PAPIER COLORS

| burnt umber | fresh foliage | licorice | metallic pure gold | sunflower | thicket | wicker white |

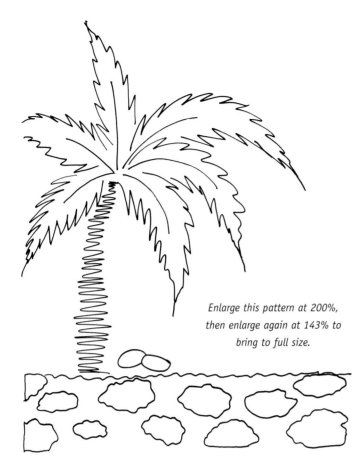

Enlarge this pattern at 200%, then enlarge again at 143% to bring to full size.

another gift idea

Paint this scene on the outside of a sturdy, solid-color vinyl bag with hefty straps, and load it with goodies to keep kids happy on a long trip. When the pint-sized beach bums reach their destination, they'll have a sack for toting around their ocean treasures.

PAINTER'S POINTER

Find an animal print you like and replicate the pattern on the bag. I liked the pattern on some tissue paper and re-created it for this project.

1 PAINT BEACH ALONG BOTTOM OF BAG

With a ruler, make a line 2" (5cm) up from the bottom of the bag to mark the beach. Put puddles of Wicker White and Sunflower on the palette. With the no. 16 flat, mix the two colors on the palette to get a lighter yellow. Basecoat the bottom of the bag with this mixture. Let the paint dry before applying detail. Don't worry about the line being perfectly straight—it will be further embellished later.

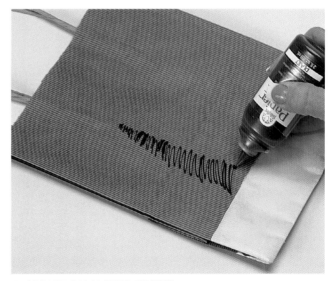

2 CREATE PALM TREE TRUNK

With Burnt Umber, begin the trunk at the top of the tree and make back and forth movements. Slightly touch the tip to the paper, but don't press too hard into the surface. As you go down the trunk, make the lines wider.

3 ADD PALM FRONDS
Make six lines with Fresh Foliage as placement for the palm fronds. Make back and forth lines, going out and in, along the placement lines.

4 SHADE FRONDS WITH THICKET
Make more lines with Thicket, right over the Fresh Foliage.

5 CREATE COCONUTS
Make two circles at the base of the palm tree with Burnt Umber for the coconuts. Fill in the circles with paint.

6 HIGHLIGHT COCONUTS
Highlight the coconuts with Sunflower, making small "C" shapes at the base of each oval.

7 ADD A WAVY LINE, PAINT ROCKS
With Licorice, paint a wavy line at the top of the ground. Using the applicator tip gives the paint fun texture. Place Burnt Umber on your palette. Using the no. 16 flat, make rock shapes on the ground with a light coat of Burnt Umber. Keep the sizes and shapes random for variety.

8 SHADE AROUND ROCKS
With Licorice and the applicator tip, make hit-and-miss outlines around each rock. Add some wiggles to the lines and keep them random.

9 HIGHLIGHT WITH GOLD
Highlight the ground line with Metallic Pure Gold, and then highlight the bottom of each rock with a wavy line of gold.

10 ADD NAME TO TAG
On the tag, pencil in the name of the recipient. Then use the applicator tip and Burnt Umber to paint in the name. Again, add some waves and wiggles to the lines as you paint.

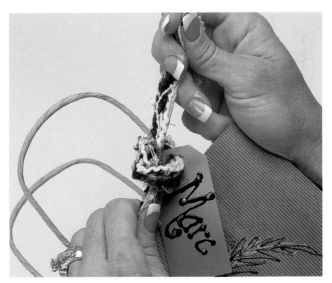

11 HIGHLIGHT LETTERS WITH GOLD
Highlight the name with gold paint to separate the letters. Also use gold to highlight the ends of each letter.

12 TIE ON TAG WITH FIBERS
Cut some fibers that match the colors in your bag to a length of 14" (36cm). Tape one end of the fibers so that you can thread them through the tag. Thread the fibers through the hole in the tag. Remove the tape and knot the fibers around the handle of the bag to secure.

SILVER WEDDING BELLS gift bag

These bags are wonderful for a formal wedding, and they show you how to create a magical, sophisticated effect using only a few colors. I used only two colors of paint—black and white—to create a very striking effect. If you're working with a different color palette, simply choose two coordinating colors that work with the bag color.

What You Will Need

7" × 9½" (18cm × 24cm) silver gift bag

wide sheer silver wired ribbon

no. 8 flat Papier brush

no. 16 flat Papier brush

Flow Medium

FOLKART PAPIER COLORS

glitter silver
sterling

licorice

wicker white

*Enlarge this pattern at 143%
to bring to full size.*

another gift idea

If your wedding gift doesn't quite fit in a bag, find some metallic solid-color wrapping paper and paint small bells and bows on the wrapped gift with white paint. Metallic reds, greens and blues are perfect colors for celebrating the holiday season.

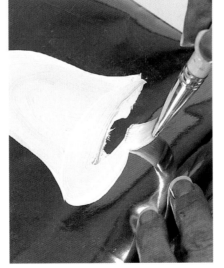

1 OUTLINE BELL SHAPE
With Wicker White on the no. 16 flat, outline the shape of the bell in the center of the bag.

2 FILL IN BELL SHAPE, ADD OVAL
Fill in the center of the bell shape with flat strokes. With more white on the brush, paint a large oval to form the bottom inside of the bell.

3 SHADE INSIDE BELL
Side load the no. 16 flat that is already loaded with white with just a tiny bit of Licorice, working it into the brush so that it looks gray. Paint the inside of the bell with this color to create the appearance of a shadow.

4 PAINT BELL'S CLAPPER

Double load the no. 16 brush with Licorice and Wicker White. Make a straight line down for the clapper, then flip the brush around to paint the ball at the end of the clapper.

5 CREATE BOW

To make the bow, start at the chisel of the no. 8 flat, pull and press down to make the wide part of the bow, and then come back up on the chisel edge.

6 ADD KNOT AND STREAMERS

Make a small "C" stroke at the top of the bell for the knot in the bow. To paint the streamer, start on the chisel edge, then press and lift to the chisel as you come down to the end of the streamer.

7 ADD ONE-STROKE LEAVES

Fill in around the bell with one-stroke leaves (see Basic Painting Techniques, page 19) using the no. 8 flat, then pull stems into the leaves with the chisel edge of the brush.

8 EMBELLISH WITH A FILAGREE

With the applicator tip, paint a random filagree pattern inside the bell. Add any additional outlining of the bell or leaves as desired.

SILVER CHAMPAGNE bag & WIRED ribbon

Enlarge this pattern at 200%, then enlarge again at 111% to bring to full size.

1 PAINT HEARTS AND BOWS

With Wicker White and the applicator tip, outline each of the hearts on the bag. Paint string bows at the top of each heart, painting streamers hanging off.

2 EMBELLISH WITH PATTERNS

Embellish each of the hearts any way you like with dots, stripes or filagree. Paint one heart with a checked pattern.

3 PULL PAINT TO FORM CHECKS

To make a harlequin pattern on the checked heart, pull the paint from the still wet stripes with the no. 8 flat to fill in every other check.

4 DECORATE WIRED RIBBON

Use Glitter Silver Sterling paint and the applicator tip to embellish a sheer satin ribbon. Paint hearts in the same way you did on the champagne bag. When using this glitter paint, the heavier you apply the paint, the more glitter that will show.

BLUE BEADED bag

The teen set will really appreciate the funky style of this fun bag. I use beaded ribbon trim and a bright color combination for a really lively presentation. Change the colors to make it appropriate for men or for the holidays.

What You Will Need

8" × 10" (20cm × 25cm) white gift bag

2½" × 4¾" (6cm × 12cm) white gift tag

no. 8 flat Papier brush

no. 16 flat Papier brush

Tip-Pen

Flow Medium

beaded white ribbon trim (TrimTations)

¼" (6mm) wide magenta silk ribbon

blue and white coordinating gift tissue

hot glue gun

glue sticks

ruler

pencil

FOLKART PAPIER COLORS

baby pink

cobalt

glitter disco

metallic blue sapphire

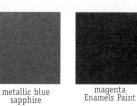
magenta
Enamels Paint

wicker white

1 DRAW A LINE ALONG BOTTOM
Measure 4½" (11cm) up from the bottom of the bag and draw a horizontal line with a ruler and a pencil.

2 PAINT STRIPES ON BAG
Load the no. 16 flat with Cobalt mixed with lots of Flow Medium, and paint vertical stripes about 2" (5cm) apart. Coming up 2" (5cm) from the bottom of the bag, paint a single horizontal stripe.

another gift idea

If you love the plaid pattern you created on this bag and tag combo, don't stop! Coordinating pieces make great gifts, so paint the front of a card with this same plaid pattern and also add it to the mat on a readymade frame. Simply insert a meaningful picture, and you have a gift that's as great as the package it comes in.

PAINTER'S POINTER
By mixing Flow Medium into the paint, you will achieve a see-through watercolor effect.

3 PAINT STRIPES ON TAG
For the tag, use the no. 8 flat to paint horizontal stripes, then vertical stripes. Place the stripes about 1" (3cm) apart.

4 PAINT WIGGLY SAPPHIRE LINES
With the Metallic Blue Sapphire paint and applicator tip, paint a wiggly line across the top of the painted section. Paint downward wiggly lines about ½" (12mm) to the right of each vertical stripe. Paint a horizontal wiggly line also.

5 ADD WIGGLY LINES IN GLITTER DISCO
Paint two horizontal wiggly lines with Glitter Disco, one on the white and one on top of the blue horizontal stripe.

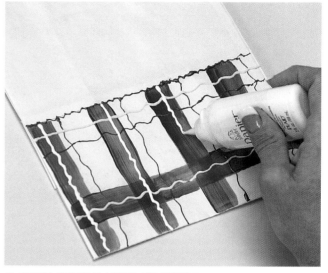

6 PAINT WIGGLY LINES IN WHITE
Paint vertical wiggly lines with Wicker White on the blue vertical stripes. Lift the tip off of the surface slightly to make nice wide lines. (For the tag, repeat the Sapphire, Glitter Disco and Wicker White stripes.)

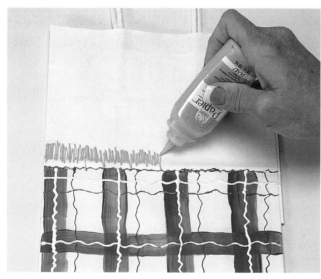

7 CREATE ZIGZAG WITH BABY PINK
Zigzag a band of Baby Pink on top of the plaid area. Let the pink dry completely before the next step.

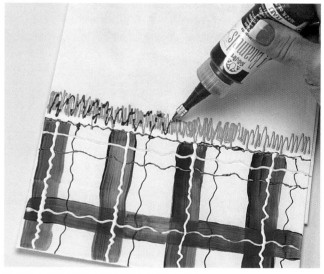

8 FOLLOW WITH MAGENTA ZIGZAG
Zigzag with Magenta using a Tip-Pen over the Baby Pink in the same manner, but using less of the Magenta.

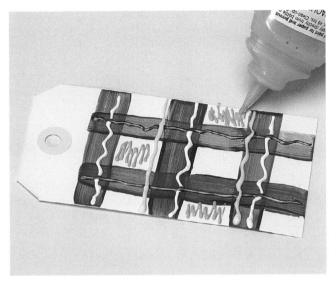

9 ZIGZAG WITH PINK ON TAG

Make horizontal wiggly lines with Glitter Disco and White on the tag. On the tag, color in every other white square with a zigzag of Baby Pink.

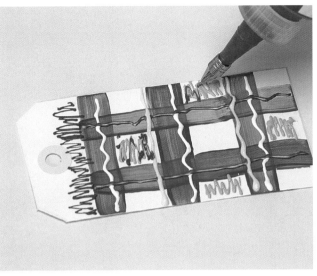

10 ADD A BIT OF MAGENTA

Zigzag a band of Magenta at the top of the tag, then add a bit of Magenta over the Baby Pink squares.

11 HOT GLUE BEADED TRIM ONTO BAG

Cut the beaded trim about 1" (3cm) longer than the width of the bag. Hot glue one end of the trim to the bag. Turn the edge of the trim over, doubling it up to get a nice finished end.

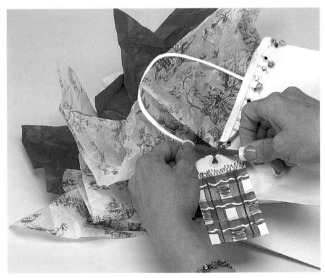

12 ADD ADDITIONAL TRIM AND ATTACH TAG

Glue the rest of the trim to the bag, running a line of glue along the top edge of the bag and placing the trim over it. Turn under the trim at the other end as well. Thread 12" (31cm) of the magenta ribbon through the hole of the tag. Tie a shoestring bow to attach the tag to the bag.

ROSES gift wrap

Wrapping a gift in roses tells your loved one that she is truly special. The fanciful pinks, blues and yellows in this gift set will make the recipient feel the renewal that comes with spring—even in the middle of winter!

What You Will Need

pearlescent white wrapping paper

4" × 2" (10cm × 5cm) light yellow gift tag

5" × 7" (13cm × 18cm) folded white card

envelope to fit card

no. 16 flat Papier brush

no. 2 script liner Papier brush

Flow Medium

¼" (6mm) wide sheer yellow ribbon

5" (13cm) wide sheer white ribbon (2 lengths, twice the height of the package, plus bow)

scissors

pencil

FOLKART PAPIER COLORS

 baby pink   dark hydrangea   fresh foliage   school bus yellow   sunflower   thicket   wicker white

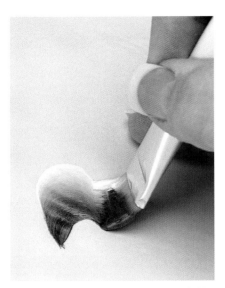

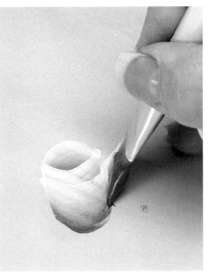

another gift idea

The look of this pretty paper is the perfect accompaniment for wedding, spring gathering or Mother's Day gifts. It also works for a baby shower because it suits boys and girls equally well.

1 MAKE AN UP-AND-OVER STROKE
Double load the no. 16 flat with Wicker White and Baby Pink paint. Watching the white edge of the brush, make a stroke up and over.

2 MAKE A U-SHAPE STROKE
Starting at the same line you began the other stroke, with the brush facing the same way, make a "U" shape. Repeat this same stroke a little bit lower, to create layers in the bud.

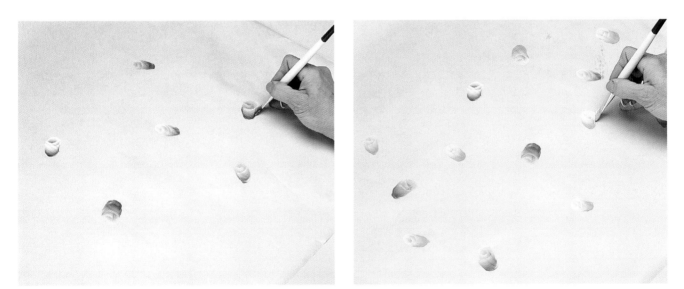

3 PAINT PINK BUDS RANDOMLY
Continue to paint pink rose buds, spacing them randomly all over the paper. Paint the buds so that they're facing in all different directions.

4 ADD BUDS IN BLUE
Double load the brush with Wicker White and Dark Hydrangea paint. Paint rose buds all around the paper, in between the pink rose buds.

5 FILL IN WITH YELLOW BUDS
Double load the brush with Wicker White and Sunflower. Fill in the rest of the space with yellow rose buds.

6 BEGIN CALYX
Double load the brush with Sunflower and Thicket. On one side of a bud, touch the brush to the surface and lean it forward.

7 FINISH CALYX
Slide the brush around the rose bud. Lift the brush to make the leaf shorter. Repeat on the other side of the bud.

8 CREATE STEM
To paint the stem, touch the brush to the surface and lean away from the bud.

9 PULL AND END STEM
Pull the stem away from the bud, lifting the brush to end the stem.

10 TOUCH DOWN TO BEGIN LEAF
To paint a leaf, touch and push down.

11 SLIDE BRUSH TO LEAF TIP
Leading with the green, slide the brush to the tip of the leaf.

12 ADD A SECOND LEAF AND STEM
Add a second leaf to the stem. Then use the chisel edge of the brush to pull a stem from the main stem into the leaf.

13 PAINT CURLICUE TENDRILS
Make inky paint with Thicket and Flow Medium, load the liner brush (see Basic Painting Techniques, page 18) and paint curlicue tendrils around the leaves and bud. Repeat for the rest of the buds.

14 ADD MORE BUDS AS NEEDED
Let the paper dry, then wrap the gift. Add any additional leaves and buds needed to make the gift look good once it's wrapped.

RIBBON bow

1 PINCH RIBBON NEAR END

Cut one length of ribbon to measure twice the circumference of the box. Trim the ends of the ribbon at a diagonal angle. Tie this ribbon around the box and tie a knot to secure. Using the ribbon that is still on the spool, measure a few inches from the end and pinch the ribbon. This "pinch" will be the center of the bow.

2 MAKE A LOOP

Make a loop with the ribbon, gathering the end toward the center.

CRAFTER'S TIP

The key to a good bow is to twist each loop before you move on to the next loop. This makes the bow full and fluffy.

3 TWIST AND HOLD AT CENTER

Twist the ribbon as you bring it toward the center, then hold the twist with the opposite hand.

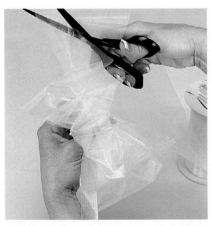

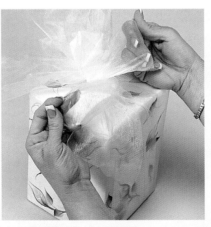

4 CONTINUE LOOPS, THEN TRIM

Continue to form larger loops with the ribbon, gathering and twisting each loop. Make more loops until you have an even number. Cut the end at an angle.

5 TIE BOW TO PACKAGE

Place the bow on the knot that is on the package. Hold the bow in place and tie a knot over the bow using the ends of the ribbon from step one. Since it is a little tricky trying to tie this knot by yourself, if you can enlist the aid of another person, by all means do so!

6 FLUFF AND SHAPE BOW

Fluff the bow by putting your fingers through the loops and pulling them apart. Trim the ends of each ribbon to the desired length. Trim the ends to a "V" shape if desired.

ROSE tag & GREETING card

1 PAINT ROSE AND NAME ON TAG
Paint a pink rose bud with calyx on the tag as directed in steps one, two, five and six for the gift wrap. Pencil the name on the tag. Paint the name with downward strokes using Thicket thinned with Flow Medium and the no. 2 script liner.

2 PAINT DOTS ON LETTERS
Dip the handle end of the no. 2 script liner into the Thicket and paint dots at the tips of the letters. For smaller dots, use the tip of a sharpened pencil.

3 ADD PINK STITCHES
Outline the edge of the card with dashes of Baby Pink using the applicator tip. The dashes will look like stitching lines.

4 THREAD YELLOW RIBBON THROUGH TAG
Cut 13" (33cm) of sheer yellow ribbon. Fold the ribbon in half and slip the loop through the hole of the tag. Place the ends of the ribbon through the loop and pull to secure the ribbon.

5 CREATE MATCHING GREETING CARD
For the card and envelope, paint on rose buds and leaves. Embellish the words with dots of Fresh Foliage. Embellish the buds with swirls of Wicker White.

FRAMED SMILING flower faces

Finding this cute pink paper with wavy checks inspired me to create cheerful, smiling flowers to peep out of a readymade frame with multiple openings. This sunny piece makes a bright impact in any child's room. Give it as a baby gift or make it for your favorite toddler's birthday.

What You Will Need

readymade frame with three 3½" × 5" (9cm × 13cm) openings

bristol board

pink, mottled scrapbook paper

⅛" (3mm) mini enamel scruffy brush

no. 2 script liner brush

no. 8 flat Papier brush

no. 16 flat Papier brush

Flow Medium

Tip-Pen

large pop dots

scissors

pencil

FOLKART PAPIER COLORS

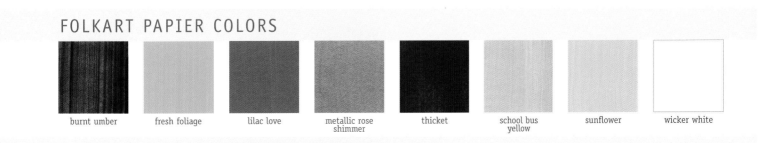

| burnt umber | fresh foliage | lilac love | metallic rose shimmer | thicket | school bus yellow | sunflower | wicker white |

Enlarge these patterns by 200% to bring to full size.

PAINTER'S POINTER
Instead of buying scrapbook paper for the background, paint your own background with a light stripe or gingham pattern.

1 TRIM PINK PAPER
Trace a piece of glass or cardboard from the picture frame onto the scrapbook paper to get the size of the picture opening. Trace a total of three, one for each opening in the frame, and cut out each piece of paper.

2 PAINT TWO YELLOW CIRCLES
Draw two circles, each about 1¼" (3cm) in diameter, on a piece of bristol board. Load the ¼-inch (6mm) scruffy with Wicker White and Sunflower. Paint each circle with the white and yellow mixture. Keep the faces of the flowers light, and set them aside to dry completely.

3 POUNCE ON CHEEKS
Using the mini scruffy brush, pounce Metallic Rose Shimmer and Wicker White onto the cheeks of each face.

4 ADD EYE SHAPES
Thin Burnt Umber to an inky consistency with Flow Medium, and dab short lines in for each of the eyes using the script liner.

5 FINISH DETAILS ON FIRST FACE
Use the same brush to paint the mouth, and to add curls for the chin, the nose and the eyebrows on the first face. Highlight the eyes with touches of Wicker White.

6 EMBELLISH WITH YELLOW DOTS
Paint the details on the second face, making him look up like he's watching for butterflies. With the Tip-Pen on School Bus Yellow, paint dots around the outside edge of the face. Set aside to let the faces dry completely.

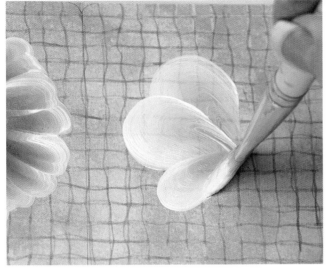

7 PAINT BUTTERFLY WINGS

For the center picture, double load Wicker White and School Bus Yellow onto a no. 8 brush on the pink paper. Paint the top wing of the butterfly, then paint the bottom wing.

8 POUNCE BUTTERFLY BODY

Using the mini scruffy brush, pounce Lilac Love and Wicker White along the edge of the wings to make the body of the butterfly.

9 OUTLINE WITH WHITE

Outline the butterfly with Wicker White using the Tip-Pen.

10 ADD DASHED LINE

Paint a dashed "fly" line near the bottom of the butterfly with white paint and the applicator tip.

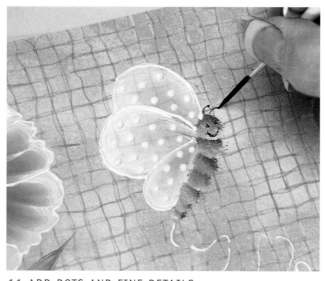

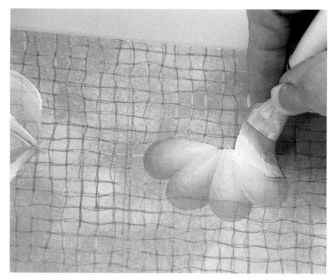

11 ADD DOTS AND FINE DETAILS
Finally, add dots to the butterfly wings with Wicker White. Then add the facial details to the butterfly with the script liner loaded with inky Burnt Umber.

12 CREATE FLOWER PETALS FOR RIGHT PICTURE
For the picture that goes on the right side, double load the no. 16 flat with Wicker White and School Bus Yellow. Keep the brush with the yellow on the outside and paint petals for a flower using the same stroke as used for the butterfly.

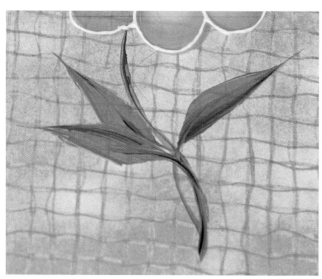

13 PULL STEMS AND LEAVES
Load the no. 8 flat with Fresh Foliage and a little bit of Thicket. Pull stems and long leaves for each of the flowers. Outline the petals of the yellow flower with Wicker White using the Tip-Pen.

14 PAINT PINK FLOWER PETALS

For the picture that goes on the left side, double load Wicker White and Metallic Rose Shimmer on the no. 16 flat. Paint shell strokes (see Basic Painting Techniques, page 23), wiggling separate shells to create the skirt of the flower.

15 ADD STEM AND LEAVES

Pull leaves and a stem, as for the yellow flower.

16 OUTLINE PETALS

With Wicker White and the Tip-Pen, outline the shell petals on the pink flower.

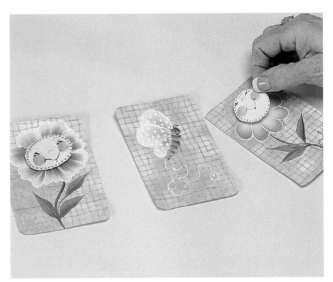

17 ATTACH FACES TO FLOWER CENTERS

Once the faces have dried, cut them out with scissors. Place pop dots on the backs of the faces, remove the backing and attach them to the flower stems painted on the pink paper squares. You're now ready to place the pictures in the frame!

EVER-BLOOMING rose

I love to find frames with all of the extra matting and trim already incuded—and you can buy them for such reasonable prices these days. This ever-blooming rose makes a really great wedding gift that symbolizes the growing love between husband and wife. Because this frame is silver with a gold tint, I've picked colors to match.

What You Will Need

11" × 14" (28cm × 36cm) readymade frame

bristol board

8" × 10" (20cm × 25cm)
warm gray cardstock

4½" × N7½" (11cm × 19cm)
warm gray cardstock

4¼" × 7" (11cm × 18cm) white rice paper
with silver flecks

¾-inch (19mm) enamel scuffy brush

no. 2 Papier script liner

no. 16 Papier flat brush

Flow Medium

Tip-Pen

ferns stencil (FolkArt One Stroke)

Xyron machine or double-sided tape

FOLKART PAPIER COLORS

linen	metallic champagne	metallic silver anniversary	thicket	wicker white

This pattern appears here at full size.

1 STENCIL BACKGROUND

Place the background stencil over the piece of 8" × 10" (20cm × 25cm) gray cardstock. Make sure to place the ferns just along the outside of the paper to create a border. Load the scruffy brush with Metallic Champagne, and pounce the paint over the stencil. Reposition the stencil each time so that the ferns are going in different directions.

another gift idea

This mature and many-layered rose would also look wonderful on a scrapbook page to accompany a scrapbooking friend's wedding picture.

2 POUNCE WITH SILVER AND GOLD

Using the scruffy brush, pounce Metallic Silver Anniversary and Champagne around the border of the 4½" × 7½" (11cm × 19cm) gray cardstock.

3 BACK GRAY CARDSTOCK

Adhere the gray cardstock to a piece of white bristol board cut to the same size. This gives the paper more weight. I used the Xyron machine to back the paper with adhesive, but you may also use double-sided tape.

4 ADHERE LAYERS TO STENCILED PIECE
Run the trimmed rice paper through the Xyron machine to make it sticky, and center it on the gray pounced paper. Run the whole piece through the Xyron machine and center it onto the stenciled piece of paper.

5 BEGIN PAINTING ROSE WITH SHELL STROKES
Double load the no. 16 flat with Wicker White and Linen. On the rice paper, paint shell strokes to start the rose (see Basic Painting Techniques, page 23).

6 ADD BUD TO CENTER OF ROSE
Paint shell strokes all around the outside skirt of the flower. Make a bud in the center, and then fill in a few more shell strokes around the bud.

7 PULL STEM
Double load Linen and Thicket on the no. 16 flat. Pull the stem from the rose down.

8 ADD A WIGGLE LEAF

To paint a wiggle leaf, start at the stem and wiggle the brush to form one side of the leaf. Turn the paper and wiggle the leaf on the other side, sliding the brush to the tip.

9 PULL THE LEAF'S STEM

To finish the leaf, pull a stem from the main stem into the leaf. Lift the brush to taper the end of the stem.

10 OUTLINE LAYERS OF ROSE PETALS

With the Tip-Pen, outline all along the edge of the flower with Wicker White, using wavy hit-and-miss outlining. Then outline the layers of ruffles inside the rose as well.

11 SIGN YOUR PIECE

Sign your painting with Thicket thinned with Flow Medium using the no. 2 script liner. Signing your work gives it extra meaning.

SCRAPBOOK
pages

scrapbooking is very popular, but it isn't just an empty fad. Before it became trendy to keep track of memories with stickers and specialty papers, archivists and devoted family historians kept records of their personal histories with what materials and resources they could scrounge up. Today, scrapbooking still serves the important purposes of tracking individuals' lives and passing on wonderful memories to future generations. Now, of course, scrapbooking has become not only a necessity but an enjoyable pastime as well. We have wonderful materials and tools available to us, and many new innovative ideas. Adding journaling to complement pictures, painting to add a personal touch and including mementos from life experiences make scrapbooking an ever more meaningful activity.

To make your pages special and unique, you can use something as simple as a card you've been given, as in the Greetings From the Past page (page 96) where I used a Mother's Day card to shape the look of the page. Another way to personalize each page is to make everything on it by hand. For instance, if you can't find the perfect paper, you can paint it. On the Oh, Baby Flowers page (page 108) I copied the flower pattern from one of my granddaughter's dresses onto a scrapbook page. You can even create your own underwater scene, like my Under the Sea page (page 116).

GREETINGS from the past

This project is all about finding a use for those numerous greeting cards you've received over the years that you couldn't bear to throw away. For this page, I cut the handwritten note from the inside of a very special Mother's Day card and attached it as journaling. I used colors from the front of the card to paint the floral design.

What You Will Need

favorite greeting card

coordinating cardstock

12" × 12" (31cm × 31cm) coordinating scrapbook paper

no. 2 Papier script liner

no. 16 Papier flat brush

Flow Medium

Xyron machine or glue stick

large pop dots

decorative-edge notch-pattern scissors

pencil

FOLKART PAPIER COLORS

amethyst   fresh foliage   glitter disco   sunflower   thicket   wicker white

Enlarge this pattern by 200% to bring to full size.

another gift idea

Don't put your shoebox full of old cards away yet—use them to make a gift for yourself. Buy a piece of glass to cover the surface of a kitchen or side table. Lay out some cards and mementos on the table top in a pleasing arrangement, perhaps even interspersing some painted and cut-out flowers among them. Simply lay the glass piece on top of the arrangement and enjoy the fruits of your sentimental nature.

1 CUT APART GREETING CARD
Cut the front off of a favorite greeting card. With decorative scissors, cut the sentiment out from the inside of the card. Set both pieces aside.

2 BEGIN PULLING PETALS
Double load the no. 16 flat with Wicker White and Amethyst. Touch the brush to the surface of the scrapbook paper, lean the brush toward the center and pull the petals for the flowers. Lead each stroke with the Wicker White side of the brush.

3 PAINT SECOND LAYER OF PETALS
Continue to paint the petals in a complete circle (see Basic Painting Techniques, page 22). Paint a part of a circle of petals for a second flower, leading with the white edge. Then paint a second layer of petals on the turned flower, leading with the dark edge.

4 PAINT MORE DAISIES

Paint the daisies on the paper as shown, or however works best to accommodate the card you choose.

5 CONNECT FLOWERS TO STEMS

Double load the no. 16 flat with Fresh Foliage and Thicket, mixing both with Flow Medium. Here the Flow Medium will allow you to make nice long strokes. Pull short lines at the base of the buds to connect the flowers with the stems.

6 PULL LEAVES OFF OF STEMS

Paint long, skinny leaves off of the stems by touching the brush to the surface and applying slight pressure (see Basic Painting Techniques, page 21).

7 PULL SLENDER STROKES

Pull a long, slender stroke as you lift to the bristles of the brush to make another leaf.

8 PULL TENDRILS

Dot the centers of each fully open daisy with the applicator tip of Sunflower. Be sure not to put the dabs too close together, as the paint will run a bit as it settles. Pull Glitter Disco tendrils around the flowers, pulling toward the main stem using the applicator tip. Arch the lines.

9 OUTLINE BOTTOM FLOWER

Outline loosely around the petals of the bottom flower, and then dot a bit of Glitter Disco in the center of this flower.

10 PAINT COMMEMORATIVE DATE

Pencil in the date next to the bottom flower. Load the no. 2 script liner with Thicket thinned with Flow Medium. To paint the numbers, touch on the surface, push down and lift up as you pull the strokes. Pull all the strokes downward to paint the date.

11 ADD DOTS TO NUMBERS

Dip the handle of the brush in Thicket and paint dots on the numbers.

12 ADHERE CARD FRONT TO PAGE

Place adhesive pop dots on the back of the front of the card, making sure to put one dot in the center so it doesn't sag. Pull the backing from the adhesives, and adhere the greeting card to the scrapbook page.

13 ADD SENTIMENT TO PAGE

Cut a piece of coordinating cardstock to a size slightly larger than the sentiment. Run the sentiment through the Xyron machine and layer the sentiment onto the cardstock. Adhere the sentiment to the scrapbook page.

GINGHAM squares

Coordinating fabrics and buttons with scrapbook paper creates interesting texture that gives a new dimension to any piece of artwork. This page was inspired by my granddaughter's birth announcement created by my son, Joel. I signed the page "Mima" especially for my new grandbaby.

What You Will Need

12" × 12" (31cm × 31cm) yellow mottled scrapbook paper

Flower Party gingham squares fabric (Donna Dewberry)

Button Its, Flower Party (Donna Dewberry)

¼-inch (6mm) enamel scruffy brush

no. 2 Papier script liner

no. 16 Papier flat brush

Flow Medium

oval stencil

⅝" (16mm) sheer apple green ribbon (the Card Connection)

adhesive dots

large pop dots

Xyron machine or double-sided tape

fine-tip permanent marker

glue stick

craft knife

FOLKART PAPIER COLORS

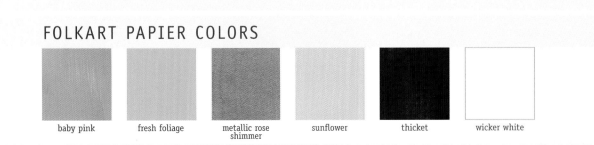

| baby pink | fresh foliage | metallic rose shimmer | sunflower | thicket | wicker white |

This pattern appears here at full size.

another gift idea

Fabric looks great on a greeting card, too. Using the same technique, cut a piece of gingham fabric to cover the entire front of a card and layer a picture on top to make a perfect greeting for a new mother's first Mother's Day.

1 PULL TWO STEMS
Load the no. 16 flat with Fresh Foliage and a little bit of Sunflower. Pull two long stems for the flowers on the scrapbook paper.

2 PAINT LEAVES
Paint long leaves on each of the stems, pushing down and sliding to a long slender tip.

3 OUTLINE LEAVES
Embellish the leaves with lines of Fresh Foliage, outlining them and adding veins.

4 PAINT BUTTERFLY WINGS

To paint the butterfly, double load the no. 16 flat with Wicker White and Metallic Rose Shimmer. Paint two large strokes for the top of the wing and two smaller strokes for the bottom.

5 POUNCE IN BUTTERFLY BODY

With the ¼-inch (6mm) scruffy, pounce Wicker White and Fresh Foliage onto the butterfly, starting at the bottom of the butterfly. Paint one segment of the body, then paint the next section so that the white and Fresh Foliage overlap and the segments are visible.

6 ADD BUTTERFLY CHEEKS

With the mini scruffy, pounce cheeks onto the butterfly with Wicker White and Metallic Rose Shimmer.

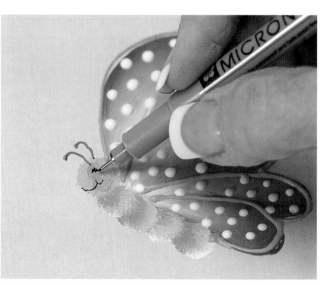

7 PAINT DOTS ON WINGS

Outline the wings with Baby Pink, making a nice smooth line. Using the no. 2 script liner, paint the antennae with Thicket thinned with Flow Medium. Then paint Wicker White dots on the wings with the tip of the bottle.

8 DRAW IN EYES AND MOUTH

With the fine-tip permanent marker, draw the eyes and a mouth.

PAINTER'S POINTER

Use a fine-tip marker anytime you don't feel comfortable using the script liner and paint for detail.

9 GLUE FABRIC TO STEM TOPS

Run a section of fabric through the Xyron machine. Cut two of the squares from the fabric and place one at the top of each flower stem.

10 ATTACH FIRST FABRIC BLOCK

Cut out a section of fabric that is two blocks wide by three blocks long (approximately 4" × 6" [10cm × 15cm]). Glue it vertically to the lower right corner of the page using the glue stick.

11 ADD PHOTOS

Cut another section of fabric to the same size as in step ten, and place it horizontally in the upper left section of the page. Trace around the pictures you'll use and cut them out (I used an oval template to give them a uniform shape). Run the pictures through the Xyron machine to make the backs sticky. Center the photos on the large sections of fabric.

12 CREATE STITCHES AROUND PHOTOS

With Fresh Foliage, make small "stitches" of dashed lines around the photos using the applicator tip.

13 ADD TEXT, BUTTONS AND BOWS TO FINISH

Put pop dots on the back of the wording, spacing them so that no areas will sag. Remove the adhesive backing. Place wording piece in the center of the page. Remove the backs from the buttons with a craft knife. Place an adhesive dot on the back of each button and attach them to the corners of the page. Cut two pieces of ribbon to about 12" (31cm) long and tie each into a shoestring bow. Place an adhesive dot on top of each photo and place a bow on each dot.

ROSE girls

The two girls featured on this page are Anna, my youngest daughter, and Renee, my oldest granddaughter. Shortly after this photo was taken, Anna left for her first year of college. I just had to make a special page for Renee to look at when she misses her aunt. Both Anna and Renee love to walk through the garden, smell the roses and watch the butterflies, so I made sure to include their favorite things on the page.

What You Will Need

roses scrapbook paper (Hot Off the Press)

sage plaid paper (Hot Off the Press)

lavender paper

favorite photo

no. 16 flat Papier brush

no. 2 Papier script liner

green leaf border sticker strip
(Me and My Big Ideas)

¼" (6mm) wide Pale Hunter ribbon
(Pure Silk)

metal charm "Love" embellishment

Flow Medium

FolkArt Papier Clear Glass Finish

blunt-nosed needle
(for stitching with ribbon)

deckle-edge ruler

scissors

tape or glue dots

FOLKART PAPIER COLORS

| fresh foliage | metallic rose shimmer | sunflower | thicket | wicker white |

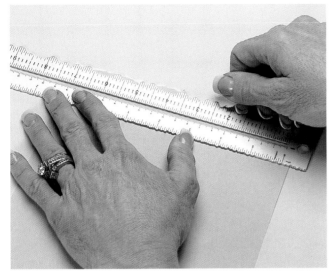

1 TEAR LAVENDER PAPER

Use a deckle-edge ruler to tear one edge of the lavender paper. Place the ruler over the paper and pull the paper upward.

another gift idea

To show a loved one that he or she is missed, you could turn this scrapbook page design into a greeting card. Simply cut out a picture of the recipient with someone who is special to her and sew on a small pocket. (You might even stick twenty dollars in the pocket as an extra treat!)

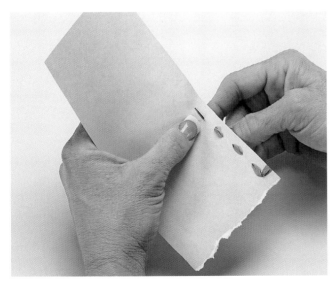

2 SEW RIBBON BORDER AROUND PAPER

Cut the other three sides of the paper to create a "pocket" that is 3½" × 8" (9cm × 20cm). Knot one end of the green ribbon. Thread the green ribbon through a large needle. Start at the back of the lavender paper near the torn edge and pull the ribbon from back to front. Pull tight, then pull the ribbon from the back to the front again with the ribbon to the side of the paper. Repeat this stitch down around three sides of the paper, knotting the top to match the other side.

3 PAINT NAMES

Paint the names or other text on the pocket using the script liner and Thicket that has been thinned to an inky consistency with Flow Medium.

CRAFTER'S TIP

If you like, you can use your sewing machine to stitch a pattern around the lavender paper, instead of sewing with the ribbon.

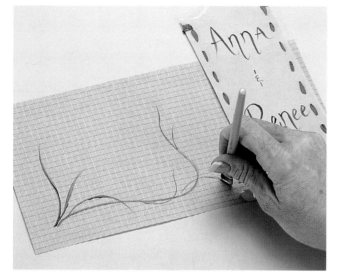

4 PULL VINES NEXT TO POCKET

Cut a piece of green plaid paper to 6" × 12" (15cm × 31cm). Place the pocket on the plaid paper for placement. Multi load the no. 16 flat with Thicket, Fresh Foliage and Sunflower. With the chisel end of the brush, pull vines in the open area next to the pocket.

5 ADD HEART LEAVES AND ONE-STROKE LEAVES

Paint heart (wiggle) leaves and one-stroke leaves on the vine (see Basic Painting Techniques, pages 19-20). Pull stems from the vines to the centers of the leaves.

6 PAINT ROSES

Double load the no. 16 flat with Metallic Rose Shimmer and Wicker White. Start the rose bud with a U-stroke, going up and over. Paint a second U-stroke to finish the bud shape, then paint small daisy strokes to fill in around the bud (see Roses Gift Wrap, page 78). Repeat across the vine.

7 PAINT CURLICUES

Load the script liner with inky Thicket and paint curlicues. Work on the tip of the brush and make loose circles.

8 CUT OUT PHOTO

Cut around the desired portion of the image in the photo with scissors.

9 ADHERE ELEMENTS TO ROSES PAPER

Adhere the painted paper to the bottom of the roses scrapbook paper. Tape the photo in place. Place a green adhesive border along the edge of the green paper, over the photo.

CRAFTER'S TIP

Glass Finish comes in the same kind of bottles as the Papier Paints and is best applied using the applicator tip. Simply squeeze the Glass Finish over the desired images (just as you would squeeze paint) to make them appear three dimensional.

10 ADHERE LAVENDER POCKET

Tape the lavender pocket onto the right side of the page, overlapping the green plaid paper. Adhere the "Love" embellishment to the painted piece using glue dots or tape.

11 EMBELLISH WITH GLASS FINISH

Pick out elements of the scrapbook paper to embellish with Glass Finish. Here I've chosen to embellish a butterfly, one bud and a rose, making them appear three dimensional. When dry, apply a second coat if you like. The result is a glass-like coating that makes the embellished elements really pop.

OH, BABY flowers

I try to find artistic inspiration everywhere. In fact, my granddaughter's dress inspired this scrapbook page. First I made a color copy of the fabric and enlarged the flowers from her dress. Then I traced the shapes to use for this page. Remember, you don't have to be Van Gogh to paint something beautiful— just keep your eyes open for unexpected inspiration and use your imagination to make it work.

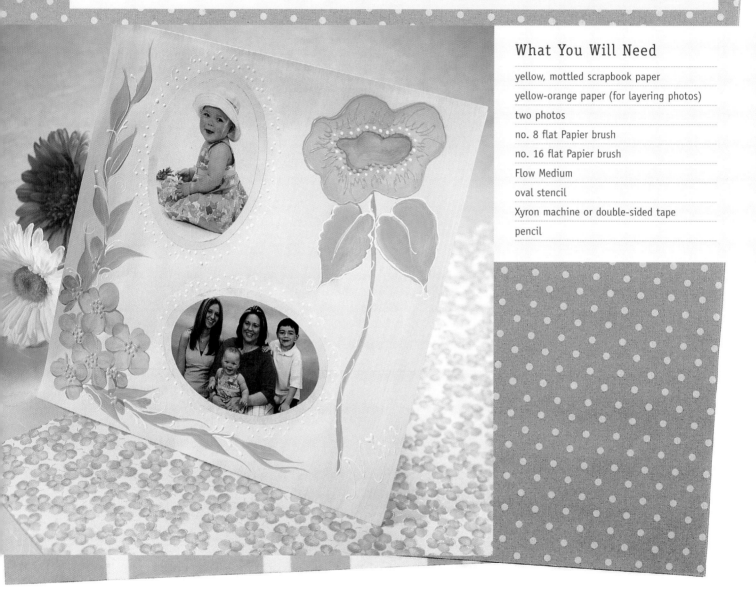

What You Will Need

yellow, mottled scrapbook paper

yellow-orange paper (for layering photos)

two photos

no. 8 flat Papier brush

no. 16 flat Papier brush

Flow Medium

oval stencil

Xyron machine or double-sided tape

pencil

FOLKART PAPIER COLORS

autumn leaves   baby pink   italian sage   school bus yellow   wicker white

Enlarge this pattern by 200%.
Enlarge again by 132% to bring to full size.

another gift idea

To make this scrapbook page into a memorable gift, simply find a frame with an oval-shaped mat in a darker color and paint white lace around the opening. Insert your favorite picture, and you'll have a gift that someone special will treasure forever.

1 PENCIL IN OVALS FOR PICTURES

Choose two photos for this page and use the oval stencil template to trace around the part of the picture you would like to use. Cut the pictures out. Use the oval template and a pencil to sketch in the photo ovals for placement on the background paper. Sketch the oval that is slightly larger than the oval you used for the photos.

2 PAINT FLOWERS

Sketch the flowers onto the background paper with a pencil or transfer the pattern from above. Double load School Bus Yellow and Autumn Leaves, adding Flow Medium, onto the no. 16 flat. Basecoat the center of the righthand flower, keeping the darker color to the outside. Load the brush with Baby Pink and Flow Medium and paint the skirt of the flower.

3 CREATE LEAVES AND VINES

Load the no. 16 flat with Italian Sage and a little bit of Wicker White mixed with Flow Medium. Paint the vines and leaves on the bottom and left of the page. To paint the long, skinny leaves, touch, press down, and then slide and lift (see Basic Painting Techniques, page 21).

4 PAINT FIVE-PETAL CLUSTERS

Double load the no. 8 flat with Autumn Leaves and School Bus Yellow. Paint five-petal flowers (see steps seven and eight in the Striped Hydrangea Card project, pages 46-47), keeping the dark color on the outside. Keep the flowers loose, painting some petals by themselves and some in clusters other than five.

5 PAINT IN LACE PHOTO BORDERS

Double load the no. 16 flat with Wicker White and Flow Medium. To paint the lace, keep the Wicker White to the outside and paint ruffled edges, keeping most of the brush outside of the pencil line as you paint. The Flow Medium will give it a transparent look.

6 EMBELLISH LACE WITH DOTS

Embellish the lace with dots of Wicker White using the applicator tip. The dots help to complete the effect of light, beautiful lace.

7 EMBELLISH WITH SWIRLS

Dot the centers of the small flowers with School Bus Yellow, using the applicator tip. With Wicker White, paint swirls and touch-pull lines around the leaves.

8 ADD DETAILS TO LARGE FLOWER

With Baby Pink, outline the skirt of the pink flower using the applicator tip. Make zigzag lines inside the pink to look like the petals are gathered. Dot Baby Pink around the outside of the orange center, spacing the dots apart so that they don't run together when the paint settles. Finally, add Wicker White outlines and dots around the stem and leaves. Be sure to sign your artwork as well.

9 ADHERE PHOTOS TO PAGE

Run the photos through the Xyron machine or use double-sided tape to adhere them to the darker yellow ovals. Tape the backs of the layered yellow ovals and adhere them to the centers of the lace ovals.

PANSY PHOTO album cover

Painting isn't just for scrapbook pages. Personalize the cover of a fabric-covered photo album with pansies, or you could even embellish the front of a favorite scrapbook with this same lovely design.

1   Double load the no. 16 flat with Violet Pansy and Wicker White, keeping the lighter paint to the outer edge. Use the flat side of the brush to paint the flowers (see Pretty Pansy Card, steps 1-3, pages 61-62).

2   Double load the no. 8 flat with Thicket and Fresh Foliage. Use the flat side of the brush to paint the leaves. Pull a stem into each leaf using the chisel edge of the brush, leading with the Fresh Foliage side.

3   Use the applicator tip to outline the flowers and add a few scrolls with Wicker White.

4   Dot the centers of the flowers using Sunflower.

5   Outline the leaves and add some curlicues with the applicator tip of Fresh Foliage.

RED flowers

In one of my granddaughter's recent pictures she is holding a red rose, and that photo inspired me to create a page to match it. When I saw this floral paper, I knew it would be the perfect background for that photo and for some painted flowers of my own.

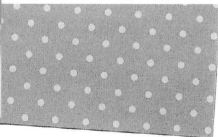

What You Will Need

red flowers scrapbook paper

green tone-on-tone pattern scrapbook paper

photos

¼-inch (6mm) enamel scruffy brush

no. 8 flat Papier brush

Flow Medium

oval stencil

wooden painted daisy

⅛" (3mm) green eyelets

metal letters for name (Making Memories)

"smile" metal word (Making Memories)

³⁄₃₂" (2mm) hole punch

eyelet-setting tool

hammer

protective surface

pop dots

Xyron machine or double-sided tape

pencil

FOLKART PAPIER COLORS

berry wine	engine red	fresh foliage	school bus yellow	wicker white

Enlarge this pattern to 154% to bring to full size.

another gift idea

Children love to look at pictures of themselves and of their family members. Create an easy gift that a toddler will enjoy now and will also cherish later by framing the entire scrapbook page and giving it to her to hang on her wall in a place where she can easily see it.

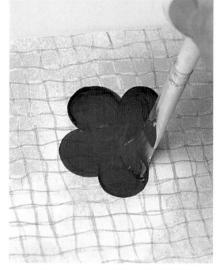

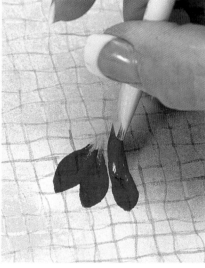

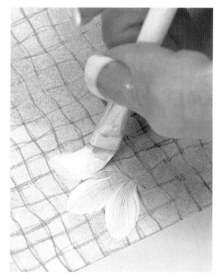

1 PAINT A FIVE-PETAL FLOWER

Cut a piece of the green scrapbook paper to 7¼" × 6" (18cm × 15cm). Double load the no. 8 flat with Engine Red and Berry Wine. Paint a five-petal flower, keeping the darker color on the outside edge (see Striped Hydrangea Card project, steps seven and eight, pages 46-47).

2 MAKE DAISY-PETAL FLOWERS

With the same brush, paint the red daisies (see Basic Painting Techniques, page 19) using the chisel edge of the brush, leading with Berry Wine. Push down as you pull the stroke to make fatter petals.

3 CREATE WHITE FLOWERS

Load the no. 8 flat with Wicker White and paint some white daisies. Use more pressure to make the strokes wider and use less pressure to make the strokes thinner.

4 ADD MORE WHITE FLOWERS

Using the applicator tip of the Wicker White paint, paint the remaining flowers by squeezing the paint starting at the outside end of the petal. Release pressure as you pull the tip toward the center of the flower.

5 PULL STEMS AND LEAVES

With the applicator tip of Fresh Foliage, pull stems from each flower to the bottom of the paper. Turn the paper upside down and pull leaves from the stem outward. Paint some of the leaves with wiggles and add veins.

6 POUNCE IN FLOWER CENTERS

Load the small scruffy with School Bus Yellow, then tap it into a bit of Engine Red. Pounce the yellow and red mixture into the centers of some of the flowers.

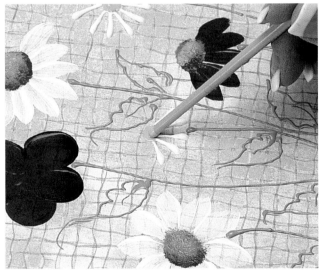

7 DOT CENTERS OF FLOWERS

Dot the rest of the centers with School Bus Yellow using the handle of the scruffy brush.

8 OUTLINE PETALS

If any of the white daisies look too transparent, like mine on the right did, outline the petals with Wicker White using the applicator tip. Outline the petals of the red five-petal flower with Engine Red.

9 ADD DOTS AROUND CENTERS

Make dots with the applicator tip of School Bus Yellow and Wicker White around the centers of the flowers.

10 PLACE DOTS IN EACH CORNER

Paint dashed lines of Wicker White around the outside of the paper. Then add dots of Engine Red in each corner of the paper.

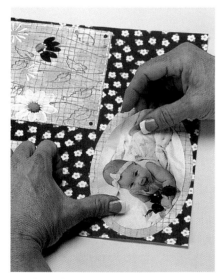

11 CUT OUT PHOTO BORDERS

Cut out green scrapbook paper borders to fit your pictures. Place them on the red scrapbook paper along with the embellished paper. Place the pictures on the border pieces using double-sided tape or by running the photos through the Xyron machine to make them sticky.

12 ADD DAISY AND LETTERS

Add the wooden daisy to the page with a pop dot and adhere the "smile" embellishment. Mark spots where you'll place the holes to attach the name letters. Make a hole with a hole punch or eyelet punch. Place the eyelet through the letter and then through the hole in the paper.

13 SET EYELETS

Turn the paper over, set the eyelet-setting tool in the hole, then tap the end of the tool with a hammer. The hammer will flare the back of the eyelet out to secure it to the paper.

UNDER the sea

This page was inspired by all of the fun photos I had of my grandkids playing in the water or just playing outside. If you want to incorporate even more photos into the page, add them in place of the fish images in the bubbles.

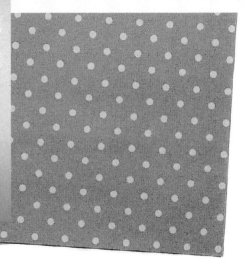

What You Will Need

12" × 12" (31cm × 31cm) blue, mottled scrapbook paper

Baby Fish Collection scrapbook paper (All Night Media)

green scrapbook paper

photos

no. 8 flat Papier brush

no. 16 flat Papier brush

Flow Medium

circle stencil

oval stencil

pop dots

double-sided tape

pencil

FOLKART PAPIER COLORS

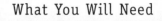

fresh foliage   glitter disco   metallic blue sapphire   wicker white

1 BEGIN PAINTING SEAWEED
Multi load the no. 16 flat with Metallic Blue Sapphire, Fresh Foliage and Wicker White, using a generous amount of Flow Medium. Paint the seaweed onto the blue, mottled scrapbook paper, pulling the stroke from the bottom of the paper up to make a curve.

another gift idea

This design may be just too cute to stay cooped up inside a scrapbook. Paint seaweed, fish and bubbles onto a large rectangle of colored cardstock or bristol board, adhere some pictures with double-sided tape so that they lay flat, and laminate both sides to make kids' placemats.

2 LEAVE SOME SEAWEED TRANSPARENT
Continue the curve at the top of the seaweed, then pull the brush back to the bottom of the page. Make some of the seaweed more transparent by adding more Flow Medium to the brush, and keep some of the seaweed opaque by adding more paint.

3 PENCIL IN RANDOM BUBBLES
With a pencil, use a circle template to draw circles of different sizes on the paper for bubbles. Scatter the circles randomly around the page.

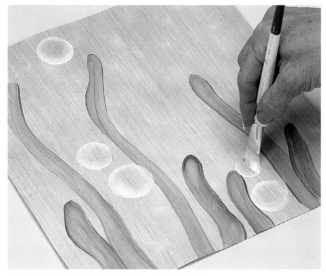

4 PAINT FIRST HALF OF A BUBBLE
Double load the no. 16 flat with Flow Medium and Wicker White. Paint the larger bubbles by first touching the brush to the surface, holding the Wicker White to the outside of the bubble, then turn it half way around to form half of the circle.

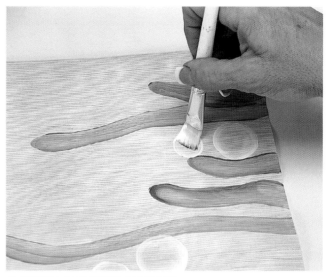

5 FINISH PAINTING BUBBLES
Flip the brush over and form the second half of the circle, keeping the white to the outside. Use the no. 8 flat to paint the smaller bubbles. Use less pressure on the brush as you paint progressively smaller bubbles.

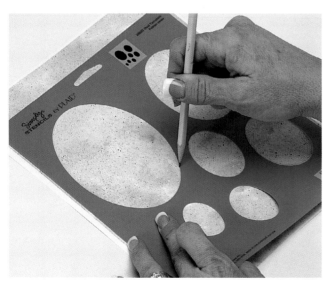

6 CUT OVALS FOR PHOTOS
Layer the pictures with green scrapbook paper. Use an oval template to make the border shape, and use it again to cut out a smaller oval shape for the photo.

7 ATTACH NAME BUBBLES

Paint the names of the children in Metallic Blue Sapphire onto a green scrapbook paper oval, dotting the ends of the letters. Use Wicker White to make a border of dots. Layer the names onto an oval of white cardstock. Cut out fish from the Baby Fish paper in circles and layer them onto white cardstock circles. Attach the names with double-sided tape and attach the bubbles with pop dots to give them dimension.

8 BRUSH ON SPARKLE

With Glitter Disco on the no. 16 flat, brush over the bubbles to give them some sparkle. The Glitter Disco will appear white when you apply it, but it will dry clear and sparkly.

SUNFLOWER pop-up card

I found a sunflower that was printed on paper and I cut it out to attach it to the front of a card. But even using pop dots I felt that it needed more depth. To add the dimension I was looking for, I painted two more sunflowers and layered them on top of the first sunflower with pop dots. Have fun experimenting with dimensional elements.

1   Paint two sunflowers, each one progressively smaller than the cut-out sunflower using the no. 8 flat. Paint one with Sunflower and Yellow Ochre and the other with School Bus Yellow and Yellow Ochre. For the centers of both flowers, use Burnt Umber mixed with Wicker White dipped in Licorice at the edge of the ½" (1cm) scruffy.

2   Attach the layered sunflowers to the card front with small pop dots.

3   Paint leaves around the layered sunflower using Thicket and Sunflower on the no. 16 flat. Outline them with Thicket.

4   With the applicator tip, paint two bees as accents, using Sunflower and Licorice for the body and Wicker White with a touch of Glitter Disco for the wings.

5   To finish, add trails for the bees and add painted stitches around the sign.

BABY DUCKS in a row

Part of the fun of scrapbooking is using "tools" as decoration. To create this bright and happy page, I used mini brass stencils as charms to complement the blue and yellow color scheme that comes from the new baby's outfit. Remember, you can use a variety of different objects to create the look you want—just think creatively.

What You Will Need

yellow scrapbook paper

aqua paper

light blue plaid paper

photos

¾-inch (19mm) enamel scruffy brush

Flow Medium

hand and footprint stickers

"Our Baby Boy" sticker (FMI)

yellow square brads (Provo Craft)

⅛" (3mm) yellow eyelets

baby items mini brass stencils (Plaid)

deckle-edge ruler

³⁄₃₂" (1mm) hole punch

eyelet-setting tool

hammer

protective surface

Xyron machine or double-sided tape

FOLKART PAPIER COLORS

 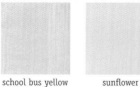

| licorice | school bus yellow | sunflower | yellow ochre | wicker white |

Enlarge this pattern by 159% to bring to full size.

another gift idea

To transform this scrapbook page into a lasting gift, add the baby's handprint and footprint to the page, as well as his birth announcement or birth certificate, and frame it for the parents to hang in the new baby's room.

1 TEAR AQUA PAPER
Measure 3½" (9cm) up from one edge of the aqua paper. Use the deckle-edge ruler to tear the paper, pulling the paper up and toward you as you tear.

2 PAINT DUCK'S HEAD
Load the scruffy with School Bus Yellow, then pounce Sunflower and Wicker White around the edge of the scruffy. Pounce the brush in a small semicircle on the aqua paper to form the head of the duck. Keep the light color to the outside of the circle to create dimension.

3 PAINT CIRCLE FOR DUCK'S BODY
Make a larger circle for the body, again keeping the lighter colors to the outside. Once you have the outer edge of the body complete, fill in the inside of the body with mostly School Bus Yellow.

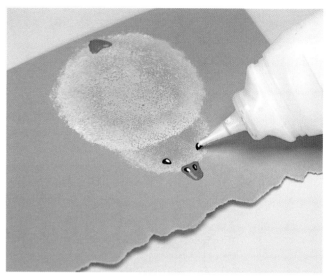

4 OUTLINE TAIL AND BEAK
Paint the duck's tail and beak with Yellow Ochre using the applicator tip. Outline both of these shapes first, then fill in the centers.

5 DOT AND HIGHLIGHT EYES AND NOSTRILS
Dot Licorice to make the eyes and nostrils, using the applicator tip. Highlight both the eyes and the nostrils with Wicker White. Let this dry for 48 hours before adhering it to the page.

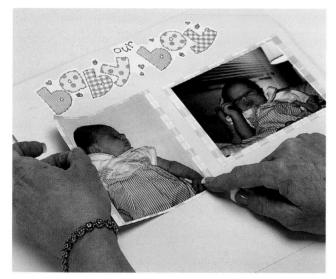

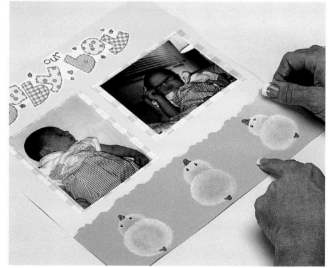

6 ADD PHOTOS TO PAGE
Place the "Our Baby Boy" sticker at the top of the page. Cut two squares of plaid paper to 5½" × 4½" (14cm × 11cm) and layer the photos on top of the plaid using double-sided tape or the Xyron machine. Tape the layered papers to the page where desired to create a pleasing layout.

7 ADHERE PAINTED STRIP
Tape the dried strip of aqua paper to the bottom of the page using double-sided tape.

8 ADD ADDITIONAL STICKERS

Place the handprint and footprint stickers in any open spaces, then place the word sticker under one of the photos.

9 ATTACH BRASS STENCIL "CHARMS"

Use the stencils as charms, and punch a hole for each one using the hole punch. Place the charm on the brad, then slide the end of the brad through the hole.

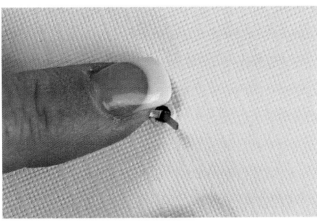

10 SECURE BRADS

Turn the paper over and open the clasps to secure the brads.

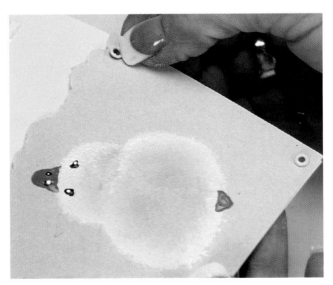

11 SET EYELETS IN AQUA PAPER

Punch holes in each corner of the aqua paper, then set yellow eyelets in the holes using the eyelet setter and hammer.

RESOURCES

All of the materials used in the projects in this book can be purchased at your local craft, fabric, scrapbooking and rubber-stamping stores or at discount department stores. If you are unable to find what you need at a local store, contact the manufacturers listed below for a retailer near you. All of the Donna Dewberry supplies are available on her website, www.onestroke.com.

CREATIVE IMPRESSIONS
2520 W. Colorado Ave.
Colorado Springs, CO 80904
(719) 596-4860
www.creativeimpressions.com
hole punches

C-THRU RULER CO.
6 Britton Drive
Bloomfield, CT 06002
(800) 243-8419
www.cthruruler.com
rulers, t-squares

DEWBERRY DESIGNS, INC.
Distribution Center
204 Hatteras Ave.
Clermont, FL 34711
(800) 536-2627
www.onestroke.com
*Flower Party gingham squares fabric,
Flower Party Button Its, ink pads, stamps*

FISKARS BRANDS, INC.
7811 W. Stewart Ave.
Wausau, WI 54401
(800) 500-4849
www.fiskars.com
scissors, deckle-edge scissors

HOT OFF THE PRESS
1250 NW Third St.
Canby, OR 97013
(800) 227-9595
www.craftpizazz.com
scrapbook papers

MAKING MEMORIES
1168 W. 500 N.
Centerville, UT 84014
(801) 294-0430
www.makingmemories.com
colored eyelets, scrapbooking accessories

PLAID ENTERPRISES, INC.
3225 Westech Drive
Norcross, Georgia 30092
(800) 842-4197
www.plaidonline.com
*Plaid Enterprises, Inc. encompasses
FolkArt, All Night Media, Brenda Walton
and Donna Dewberry supplies, including
Papier paints, FolkArt One Stroke brushes
and Flow Medium*

POSH IMPRESSIONS
22600-A Lambert St., Ste. 706
Lake Forest, CA 92630
(800) 421-7674
www.poshimpressions.com

WACKYTAC, LLC
Parkville, MO 64152
(913) 221-1729
www.wackytac.com
pop dots, dimensional adhesives

happy painting and papercrafting!

I HOPE THE PROJECTS IN THE BOOK HAVE INSPIRED YOU TO KEEP CREATING PERSONALIZED ARTWORK OF ALL KINDS.

INDEX

A-B
Adhesives, 12
Baby shower, 27, 79
Beach scene, 66-69
Birth announcements, 32-35, 41
Bows, 72, 82
Brushes, 13
  cleaning, 14
  loading, 16-18
  roller, 31
  script liner, 13, 18, 88, 102
  scruffy, 13, 17, 36-39
Butterflies, 26-31, 37, 84-85, 87-89,
  100-103

C-D
Cards, 25-63, 105
  birthday, 50-51
  Easter, 40-42
  of encouragement, 37
  fabric, 101
  get well, 36-39
  Halloween, 43
  just-a-note, 52-55
  pop-up, 119
  re-using, 96-97
  season's greetings, 43
  sympathy, 46
  thank you, 53
Cards, floral
  hydrangea, 44-48, 56-59
  lilac, 50-51
  pansy, 60-63
  rose, 83

Caterpillar, 36-37, 39
Chalk, 35-36, 38-39, 51, 57-59
Charms, 11, 120, 123
Colored pencils, 50-51, 58
Cup, party, 30
Ducks, baby, 27, 120-123

E-F
Easter eggs, 40-42
Embellishments, 11
  buttons, 100, 103
  fibers, 63, 66, 69
  googly eyes, 34, 39
  ribbon, 11, 52, 55, 58, 73-74, 77, 105
  yarn, 32, 34, 36, 39
Embossing, 10, 41, 53-54
Envelopes, lining, 60, 63
Fabric, 100-101, 103, 108-111
Fish, 27, 32-35, 116, 119
Flow Medium, 13, 18, 75, 81, 98, 109-110
Flowers, 13, 19, 84-86, 89
  daisies, 22, 96-99, 112-115
  five-petal, 46-47, 49, 110, 113-114
  hydrangea, 44-48, 56-58
  lilac, 50-51
  pansies, 60-63, 111
  roses, 78-81, 83, 90-93, 104, 106-107
  sun-, 119

G-I
Gift bags, 27, 30, 65-77
Gift wrap, 49, 51, 65, 71, 78-81
Gifts, framed, 75, 84-93, 109, 113

Glass Finish, 107
Greeting cards, 96-97, 101, 105
  See also Cards
Invitations, party, 26-28, 61

L-N
Leaves, 13, 45, 88, 101, 114
  heart, 20
  long, skinny, 21, 98, 110
  one-stroke, 19, 21, 46, 62, 72
  rose, 81
  smooth, 21
  stamped, 52, 54
  stenciled, 44-45
  wiggle, 93
Mother's Day, 79, 101, 109
Names, adding, 83, 105, 112, 115, 119
  See also Words, adding
Nametags, 69, 77, 83
Napkin ring, 30

P
Paints, 13, 15, 18, 47
Palm tree, 66-68
Paper, 11, 14, 23
Patterns, 14
  animal print, 67
  beach scene, 67
  butterflies, 27, 85, 101
  caterpillar, 37
  daisy, 97
  ducks, baby, 121
  fish, 33

FIND CREATIVE inspiration and instruction IN OTHER FINE NORTH LIGHT AND MAKING MEMORIES BOOKS!

THESE BOOKS AND OTHER FINE TITLES ARE AVAILABLE FROM YOUR LOCAL ART & CRAFT RETAILER, BOOKSTORE, ONLINE SUPPLIER OR BY CALLING 1-800-448-0915.

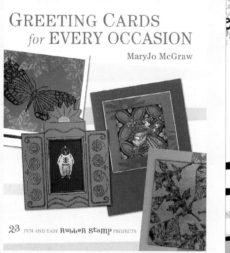

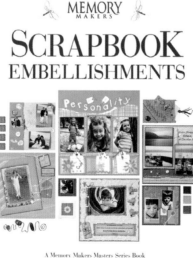

GREETING CARDS FOR EVERY OCCASION

Create heartwarming, handcrafted cards for every occasion! Inside *Greeting Cards for Every Occasion*, you'll find basic techniques, tips and guidance for crafting personalized greeting cards for your all of your family members and friends. Each project features clear step-by-step instructions that show you how to use stamps, decorative paper and other easy-to-find materials to make handcrafted cards that are works of art. Plus, you'll discover MaryJo McGraw's gallery of ideas for making inspired cards to celebrate the special events in your life.

ISBN 1-58180-410-5, paperback, 128 pages, #32580-K

CREATING CARDS WITH SCRAPBOOK EMBELLISHMENTS

In her latest book, MaryJo McGraw brings the hottest scrapbooking techniques to the world of handcrafted cards. She makes it fun and easy for papercrafters and scrapbookers to work with stunning 3D embellishments to craft creative, elegant cards. With 26 step-by-step projects and more than 40 variations to choose from, crafters of all skill levels will find inspiration. The book also includes a handy "Getting Started" section that covers all of the basic materials and techniques.

ISBN 1-58180-628-0, paperback, 128 pages, #33201

PAPERCRAFTING ROOM BY ROOM

Today's papercrafters want intriguing paper projects beyond just cards and gifts, and a growing trend is using this super-hot medium to turn ordinary home items into extraordinary pieces. In this premier book, Deborah Spofford shows you how to make stylish accents for every room in your home. *Papercrafting Room by Room* features over 26 step-by-step demonstrations for creating or enhancing popular household objects, including instructions on how to use paper to embellish everything from lampshades, tabletops and plates to mouse pads, clocks and more.

ISBN 1-58180-656-6, paperback, 128 pages, #33243

SCRAPBOOK EMBELLISHMENTS

Make scrapbook pages come to life using the embellishment techniques of 10 of the world's top scrapbookers. Find inspiration for using decorative embellishments to turn an average page into one that dazzles. In *Scrapbook Embellishments*, 10 Memory Makers Masters offer inspiration and direction for enhancing scrapbook pages with embellishments that feature the latest products and techniques. You'll find dozens of diverse examples covering a variety of themes that will show you how to create 150+ sensational scrapbook pages using textiles, organic materials, metal, paper and more!

ISBN 1-892127-31-8, paperback, 128 pages, #32998